Education, Health and Citizenship

Education, Health and Citizenship

Three Dimensions of Empowering Adolescents

Edited by
Vijay Shankar Vyas

Ajit Foundation, Bikaner

RAWAT PUBLICATIONS
Jaipur • New Delhi • Bangalore • Guwahati • Kolkata

ISBN 978-81-316-0998-9

Published by
Prem Rawat for **Rawat Publications**
Satyam Apts., Sector 3, Jawahar Nagar, Jaipur 302 004 (India)
Phone: 0141 265 1748 / 7006 Fax: 0141 265 1748
E-mail: info@rawatbooks.com
Website: www.rawatbooks.com

New Delhi Office
4858/24, Ansari Road, Daryaganj, New Delhi 110 002
Phone: 011-23263290

Also at *Bangalore, Guwahati* and *Kolkata*

Typeset by Rawat Computers, Jaipur
Printed and bound in India

Content

Foreword

At the outset, I would like to thank Prof. Vyas and the team of *Ajit Foundation* for facilitating this opportunity to bring together a collective of expertise and experience and singularly focus on discussions on 'adolescents empowerment'. As we all know, this is clearly one of the most important and vital subjects to India's growth and development.

India is one of the youngest nations in the world, with more than 54 per cent of the total population below 25 years of age. When you juxtapose this with some state-level statistics of Rajasthan—where about one-fourth of the population[1] belongs to 10–19 years' age group, you realise the enormity of this demographic dividend.

However, a glance at the social milieu around us confirms that for a large majority, this second decade of childhood ceases to exist under the burden of adulthood that is thrust on adolescents. Seven of 10 girls would have dropped out of education by VIII standard. One out of three would be married before she crosses 18 years.

With societal norms and pressures, it is only a matter of time when a girl puts her life at stake for motherhood. Evidence on the ground begs the questions: Who is an adolescent and what is his or her empowerment?

World Health Organization identifies adolescence as the period in human growth and development that marks the phase of transition from childhood to adulthood, which coincides with 10–19 years, which is a transition in all forms: physical, psychological, emotional, social, cultural, and economic.

Often addressed as 'the emerging generations', if given the right environment and opportunities, adolescents have the potential to become change makers and not just passive beneficiaries.

However, there are several issues that adolescents in the state are faced with today, which act as bottlenecks. Some of these issues are inadequate nutrition, child marriage, incomplete education, early pregnancy and child care, sexual and reproductive health, violence and abuse, child labour, and inadequate skills to earn a decent living.

Notably, these issues are not mutually exclusive subsets. Furthermore, it is interesting to note that when you go out into the villages and hold community meetings on these issues, there is hardly any participation from amongst adolescents. This in itself highlights the complexity of adolescent empowerment.

As an organisation, United Nations Children's Fund (UNICEF) has been working on some of these very complex issues. Our focus is to work with the most fragile, the most vulnerable adolescents and help them overcome inequity and to grow and become empowered. Our work and deliberations with the government, other UN agencies, and experts in the field have generated some pointed needs.

The first is the need for more specific disaggregated evidence on adolescent health, nutrition, water sanitation, and hygiene, including menstrual hygiene, education and child protection, and studies on norms and social dynamics. Second is an urgent deliberation on what are some of the critical issues that policy and decision makers need to prioritise. Some of these issues could be:

1. The need for one nodal department to manage and coordinate adolescent programming across departments and flagships;
2. Ways in which comprehensive policy documents can be enabled with operational modalities to turn them into realities; and
3. Mechanisms for participation of adolescents in decision-making and mechanisms to reach voices of adolescents to policymakers. Especially the voices of the most marginalised, the ones who are shadowed under the overwhelming culture of silence and invisibility.

India enshrines its welfare objectives in a dedicated section in the constitution, called the Directive Principles of State Policy. In other words, the government leads all development mandates from the front. It is for all of us to come together to support the accomplishment of the development agenda for the future generation.

It is in recognition of this that, as I wind up, I would like to make two requests to this group:

1. Create a participatory roadmap for working with adolescents, which should essentially have health and development-specific standards outlined for the growth of adolescents. This could then be broken down into timelines and geography-specific benchmarks. To this end, an Inter-Agency Group could be constituted, under the leadership of the government.
2. Suggest a war-footing, fast-track-model mechanism[2] to start achieving identifiable, definite results in a short time frame as well as lay the platform for a longer programme implementation, of course, without compromising the critical aspects of equity and inclusiveness.

On behalf of UNICEF, I would like to assure all possible support towards the realisation of the full potential of this vibrant age of adolescence that would one day write the future of this nation.

I wish the very best to all participants for a successful and fruitful two-day consultation on adolescent empowerment. Thank you!

Isabelle Bardem-Sévédé, PhD
Chief Field Officer, UNICEF, Rajasthan

Notes

1. Based on the opening speech in Consultation on Adolescent Empowerment: Policy and Practice, 4 December 2017, Jaipur.
2. The fast-track model is a model that was pioneered in the for-profit sector in the United States and Europe, as also in India. The model outlines a 90–120-day period for achievement of smart outputs. In the development sector, this has been tried successfully in many themes across many African countries.

Acknowledgement

The papers contained in this volume were presented in a consultation on empowering adolescents. The consultation was organised by Ajit Foundation in collaboration with UNICEF and United Nations Population Fund (UNFPA). We are grateful to the UNICEF state programme coordinator Dr Isabelle Bardem and her colleague Manjaree Pant and UNFPA state coordinator Sunil Jacob for their continuous support. We thank Isabelle for giving a stimulating opening speech to the consultation, which is published as the Foreword of this volume.

We are obliged to the authors of all the papers included in this volume, who presented their views and findings on different aspects of adolescents in a clear and effective way. These papers were discussed by panels of subject-matter specialists. For meaningful discussions in panels, we are thankful to our learned colleagues, Sharda Jain, Prabhat Pankaj, and Ajay Singh Mehta, chairpersons of the panels, and the members of the panels for their valuable contribution during discussions.

We would like to thank all the participant organisations, knowledgeable stakeholders, and particularly the group of articulate adolescents coming from diverse background for their active and thoughtful participation.

For reporting the proceedings of the consultation, we are thankful to Dr Anju Dhadda Misra, Sapana Nehra, and Geeta Garwa and to Kalyan Singh Kothari for preparing notes for the press. We are thankful to Sadhana Garg who picked up the work of copyediting of the papers in an efficient way at a short notice.

We would like to give credit for organising the consultation and attending to all chores in a satisfactory way to the team comprising Laxmi Vyas, Amit Kumar, Rajesh Sharma, Sanjay Shrimali, and Ganesh Sharma.

Special thanks to Mr Pranit Rawat of Rawat Publications for taking personal interest in bringing out this book in a short time and for his thoughtful suggestion to make the publication a befitting volume in subject matter as well as in presentation.

We are grateful to all those who helped us in organising the consultation and in bringing out this volume. We do hope that they would agree that they, in their own ways, contributed to this effort towards the empowerment of adolescents, which is the crying need of our time.

Thank you all!

V.S. Vyas
Chairman, Ajit Foundation

Contributors

Vijay Shankar Vyas (vijaysvyas2108@gmail.com) is Chairman of Ajit Foundation, an institution working for the past two decades for empowering youth. He has a PhD in economics and has taught at Mumbai University, Sardar Patel University, and Indian Institute of Management, Ahmedabad. He was awarded DLitt (honoris causa) by Maharana Pratap University of Agriculture Sciences, Udaipur. He was a member of Prime Minister's Economic Advisory Council, member of the central board of Reserve Bank of India, and Deputy Chairman of the State Planning Board of Rajasthan. He was awarded *Padma Bhushan* in 2006 by the President of India.

Abhinav Pandya (pandya.abhinav@gmail.com) has a master's degree in Public Administration from Cornell University (USA). He has worked as a member of a Specialist Team of International Labour Organisation (UN) on Mahatma Gandhi National Rural Employment Guarantee Scheme. Currently, he serves as strategic advisor to Vidya Bhawan Sansthan, Udaipur, Rajasthan. He regularly writes on foreign policy issues and youth affairs.

Pratham (kbkothari@gmail.com) is a civil society institution working for the quantitative improvements in education and providing access to education to the deprived sections of the society. The paper in the volume has been prepared by Pratham team working with Pratham Open School and their e-learning group.

Shobhita Rajgopal (shobhita@idsj.org) is Associate Professor at the Institute of Development Studies, Jaipur. She has over two decades of experience in social development research, training, and policy advice with special emphasis on women's rights, gender, and development and mainstreaming gender concerns in policy planning and implementation. She has published extensively on gender perspectives.

Pawan Gupta (pawansidh@gmail.com) is the founder of the Society for Integrated Development of Himalaya (SIDH), Uttarakhand. Inspired by Gandhian philosophy in education and in rural development, SIDH is conducting experiments in the rural areas of Himachal Pradesh to make education more meaningful and relevant.

Narendra Gupta (narendra@prayaschittor.org) is a community health physician and serves as an adviser to the civil society organisation Prayas. Based in Chittorgarh, he works on citizen-centric research, planning, and execution of community-based healthcare programmes to mobilise right to healthcare and free universal access to essential and life-saving medicines and diagnostics.

S. Ramanathan and Vasudha Chakravarthy (sramanathan@devsolutions.org) are both partners at Development Solutions, a research and consultancy organisation based at New Delhi. Ramanathan has 30 years of experience in research and programme management on issues of health and livelihood. Vasudha, an MPH, has been working on issues of reproductive health, health systems, and gender over the past seven years. She was one of the ten global fellows selected by the Maternal Health Task Force, Harvard

School of Public Health to undertake research on maternal health.

Kanchan Mathur (kanchanmathur10@gmail.com) is Professor at the Institute of Development Studies, Jaipur. She has over 30 years of experience in applied research, evaluation, and policy analysis in the field of social and rural development, especially focussing on gender issues. She has published extensively in journals of national and international repute. She has wide-ranging experience of working with national and international organisations. Her current areas of interest include understanding the politics of gender cutting across sectors, gender mainstreaming, gender and rural local governance, and women's issues.

Jayshree Godara (jayshreegodara@gmail.com) is a lecturer in Home Science College of Rajasthan Agricultural University. She was closely associated with *Ajit Foundation*'s programme of empowering adolescent girls and had been coordinator of the adolescent girls' empowerment camps of the same organisation.

Malavika Pavamani (malavika.pravah@gmail.com) has been associated with Pravah since 2011. Malavika is currently the co-director of the Adolescent Intervention team of youth and facilitators. She has anchored Pravah's instructional design and facilitation training programmes. She was a trainer with the British Council change maker's network and has been among the delegates representing India for the Commonwealth Youth Programme in South Africa. **Neha Buch** and **Ishanee Bhattacharyya** are her colleagues in Pravah.

Navendu Mishra (navendum12@gmail.com) is a co-founder of Agrini in Madhya Pradesh. Agrini works on propagating values propagated in the Indian Constitution among the youth. **Gaurav Jaiswal** is his colleague at Agrini.

Monisha Vemavarapu (monisha@rubaroo.org) is a co-founder of Rubaroo, Hyderabad. Rubaroo encourages fellow feeling among the youth and helps them to understand basic values propagated by different religions in order to promote communal harmony. **Hema Khatri, Neha Swain, Shubhi Dwivedi** and **Balendu Rashmi** are her colleagues in Rubaroo.

1

Introduction

V.S. Vyas

Adolescent boys and girls, in the age group of 10–20 years roughly, are in a difficult period of their lives. They are in a transitional phase from childhood to adulthood and suffer from uncertainty and anxiety on various counts. They are bothered about changes in their body, confused about the subjects they should pursue for higher studies, and are not aware of the rights and wrongs in dealing with people. Girls are in a particularly disadvantaged position, as are boys and girls from the marginalised sections of our society.

Issues facing the adolescents need to be seen in the context of a fast-changing socio-economic milieu and the accompanying technological changes that affect their health, education, social behaviour, and future prospects profoundly. The social media in its various forms is now a game-changer. Its impact is clear on the so-called modern India; it is also progressively extending its reach to the more traditional Bharat. The distinction between India and Bharat is anyway becoming blurred rapidly in the wake of the spread of transport, communication, and internet facilities. This has changed the contours of the old and persistent issues the adolescents face.

The most worrisome among these are health-related issues. Unfamiliar bodily changes cause severe anxiety, especially to girls. This is compounded by an ignorance of reproductive health. Such ignorance creates lifelong handicaps in regions where child marriage is commonplace. Another widely prevalent health issue is malnutrition, oftentimes in the more affluent sections as well. Surveys show iron deficiency among girls from rural as well as urban areas, and poor as well as rich families. Naturally, these problems also lead to worry and anxiety among all adolescents to a major or minor extent.

Anxiety and pressure to compete in education and in social space reach destructive levels among the youth. The reintroduction of examinations at various stages in the primary and secondary education has replaced the joy of learning with a rat race to increase marks and improve grades. The situation is aggravated by pressure from the family and other well-wishers. The compulsion to meet the norms of modern lifestyle as depicted in films, television, and social media is even more intense. The peer group becomes the referral point, and a failure to measure up to the desired standards becomes a potent source of anxiety possibly leading to health and behavioural problems.

Girls and boys now have access to primary education practically all over the country, although in some pockets, universal primary education is not yet a reality, especially for girls. But present trends indicate that these gaps will be covered in the foreseeable future. The main problem is the poor quality of education. Many knowledgeable persons have given a lot of thought to it. We at *Ajit Foundation* have discussed this aspect in great detail in an earlier consultation on *Right to Education: The Next Phase*. *Right to Education: The Next Phase* was edited by V.S. Vyas and Anju Dhadda Mishra and published by *Ajit Foundation*, Bikaner 2015.

Most adolescent girls and boys today face problems related to post-primary education. Secondary education facilities, especially in public (government) schools, are woefully inadequate. As it so often happens in scarcity situations, the poor and marginalised are left on their own, whereas children from better-off families attend better equipped private schools. Even where adequate facilities are available, the type of education provided does not always equip the students to pursue further education in a meaningful way, nor does it prepare them adequately for gainful employment. Vocational training is virtually absent from the curricula. Those who can afford to pursue higher education do so without any assessment of their career prospects or capabilities. There is no system of counselling and mentoring. Students end up having to rely on the advice of their parents or peers. The upshot is that students often realise that they made a wrong choice after completing their studies.

Adolescent development, whether in the family or school, should lead to inculcating values of good citizenship, namely equality, non-discrimination, and empathy for the disadvantaged. Neither the present social environment nor education places the needed stress on these values. The adolescent imbibes consumerism and self-centred pursuit of happiness as desirable virtues in the current competitive environment. Boys are encouraged to be aggressively masculine and girls to develop a sense of dependence and coy femininity. Social organisations aggravate the problems instead of countering these tendencies. Continued prevalence of gender inequality and discrimination, child marriage, and dowry are results of social pressures driving the families to take decisions injurious to the welfare of the girls and boys.

It is time not to repeat tales of woes the adolescents face but to address constructively these challenges and find some solutions. A number of scholars have given serious thought to these issues. Many social institutions have rich experience of taking practical measures at the community level to address these problems. We also have some government policies and interventions aiming to set the course right. These thoughts and experiences of all the stakeholders need to be shared, to identify missing links and common threads that may be useful in formulating an integrated approach to adolescents' problems. *Ajit Foundation* recently organised a consultation involving representatives of all stakeholders precisely with this objective. This volume contains some of the papers presented at the consultation.

As in the past two consultations, *Right to Education: The Next Phase* and *Building Blocks for a Youth Policy*, edited by V.S. Vyas and Shreekant Sambarani, published by Academic Foundation, New Delhi (2017), the discussion in this consultation too was based on theme papers by experts who have given deep thought to these issues and have some constructive opinions to offer. This introduction is a brief account of the issues and approaches advocated by the scholars and practitioners.

Abhinav Pandya in his paper 'Education and Citizenship' maintains that education should be taken as an end in itself, as it is more than a means to equip students for earning their livelihoods. He focusses on education for preparing youth for active citizenship. He highlights the gaps in the present education system. The major problem is that the system kills the spirit of enquiry. The author suggests that a study of philosophy at an early stage will help. He also argues that the classification of subjects in water-tight compartments such as science, commerce, and arts, should be done away with. Instead there should be a cross-disciplinary curriculum. After observing student union elections in an educational institution, he concludes that student politics is misleading the youth by mirroring the corruption and opportunism in the local-, assembly-, and parliament-level elections. Debasement of the quality of academics is another of his concerns. He recommends working on the mental and physical health of students who face crippling and debilitating problems from stress, frustration, depression, and anxiety. He suggests that this can be done through *yoga, pranayam,* and meditation, which should form parts of the curriculum. He emphasises the importance of spiritual and moral values in education.

The *Pratham* case study 'Second Chance' probes the reasons for the high dropout ratio at school level. It groups dropouts into two categories, namely dropouts due to low level of learning ability making it difficult for students to cope with the education in the higher standards, and social, cultural, and economic reasons, which come in the way of continuing schooling. *Pratham* has designed location-specific flexible programmes to attract the dropouts back into the mainstream of education. The paper concludes that a uniform policy will not work for heterogeneous groups with diverse needs. The paper indicates that the *Pratham* programmes have met with commendable successes.

Shobhita Rajgopal traces the history and spread of the *Doosara Dasak* programme of Rajasthan in a case study ('Adolescent Learning and Empowerment Education'). The programme aimed at providing education to dropouts, especially from the marginalised sections, through residential camps which provided training using an integrated curriculum. It also aimed to harness the energies of the adolescents for social change. The author notes that social mapping and micro-planning have proved very useful in identifying the problems of dropout children as well as those faced by the community, and in designing appropriate initiatives. She discusses the relative importance of the various components of the programme, namely, residential camps, continuing learning centres, women's groups, youth groups and resource groups. She also points out some of the challenges the programme faced at the ground level. They include ensuring community ownership and involvement, sensitising local institutions, mobilising men and materials for resource intensive activities, scaling up the programme and, measuring the outcome. Exposure to technology, resultant changes in life style and consumption patterns have now become characteristic features of this age group. Earning easy money in a short time is becoming an important objective. The programme has to cope with these new generation problems.

Pawan Gupta discusses the approach to education by *Society for Integrated Development of Himalayas* (*SIDH*) ('An Approach to Existential and Integrated Education for Youth'). The Society's work is inspired by *nai taleem*, a pedagogy advocated by Gandhi and Vinoba. It is an integrated approach to the teaching and learning process, and structured around constructive, productive, creative hands-on work. Learners are helped to understand the concepts of values, ideas and objects, all the time emphasising intrinsic understanding and experiential learning by the students. *SIDH* keeps the objective of learning centre-stage and weaves the subjects around it, constructing an integrated method of acquiring knowledge rather than gathering information. This method instils confidence in the learner. In its school, subjects such as mathematics, science, environment, agriculture, health, hygiene, economics and even world politics are taught in conjunction with physical work, compulsory for all students. Projects are designed to develop understanding of regional knowledge, culture and ethos. Students are made to understand and appreciate them. The idea is to give students confidence through genuine understanding and knowledge and liberating them form mere appearances. In the process, students begin to appreciate what is good and worthy in their own culture and local knowledge systems. The author feels that *SIDH* provides an alternative approach to conventional schooling, emphasising value-based learning deeply rooted in the local context and sharing local knowledge as the building blocks.

Papers and case studies on health comprise two theme papers, by Narendra Gupta and S. Ramanathan (with Vasudha Chakravarthy), and two case studies, of Jatan Sansthan and the *Ajit Foundation* programme of adolescent girls' camp. Gupta gives an overview of health situation of adolescents in India, encompassing reproductive, sexual, mental and nutritional health ('Health Concerns of Adolescents in India'). He provides historical background to show how the health concerns of adolescents started receiving attention of policy makers over a period of time. He cites all-India surveys and studies to depict the situation as it has evolved and makes important suggestions for moving forward. Ramanathan and Chakravarthy focus mainly on important government policy and programmes ('Policies and Programmes on Adolescent Health in India'). They classify existing programmes into three categories: community-based intervention (*Kishori Shakti Yojana*), school-based interventions (adolescent education programmes of the Human Resource Development ministry) and health-system based intervention (adolescent reproductive and sexual health programme). They list the main reasons for policies and programmes not being very successful. These can be grouped into attitudinal issues, implementation issues and coordination issues. The most serious flaw is that the policies appear to be made in view of the needs of the systems and/or the administration and not for the adolescents.

Kanchan Mathur presents a case study of Jatan Sansthan ('Supporting Adolescents' Sexual Health and Rights'). It traces the 16-year journey of this community-based organisation located in Rajasmand district of Rajasthan. The study analyses the two major components, *Hillor* and *Uger*. The first addresses issues of early marriage, school dropouts and skill empowerment. It aims to raise social consciousness of reproductive health, as well as enabling adolescents to generate economic assets. It recognises local realities in an effort to assess the nature and extent of the problems and designs its approach accordingly. The second project, *Uger,* meaning new beginning, addresses the menstrual health of girls and women. It aims to dispel the myths and apprehensions around menstruation, which affect not only the health and well-being of the girls but also their self-image. The study lists the lessons Jatan Sansthan learned by experience and appreciation of ground realities, which could be replicated elsewhere in Rajasthan.

Jayshree Godara traces the history of *Ajit Foundation,* an NGO working with youth in Bikaner (Rajasthan) since 1994 and describes its vision, mission and main programmes ('Empowering Adolescent Girls'). A key initiative is a four-day non-residential camp for adolescent girls. It is a comprehensive programme focussing on health. It also looks into other aspects of adolescent girls' lives in a traditional society. The main objective is to impart essential knowledge to boost the self-confidence of adolescent girls enabling them to face realities of life. Physical and psychological changes accompanying adolescence, nutritional needs of adolescents, the contributions of education and law to women's empowerment and challenges before women in their various roles and positive thinking for facing them are among the concerns discussed in these camps. Mothers of participating girls are also invited to some camps. Visits to institutions relevant for girls, such as family courts, lady police stations, newspaper offices and radio and television stations is an innovative feature of the camps. Nearly 1,000 girls have participated in these camps so far. An evaluation by an external expert suggests that the objective is largely met.

Chapters ten to twelve contain three case studies of organisations aiming to make adolescents responsible citizens. The first by Malavika Pavamani and her colleagues from *Pravah* ('Nurturing Lifelong Active Citizens: A 5th Space Approach'), defines citizenship as a 'journey from blaming to claiming'. The objective is sought to be achieved by creating a space (fifth space), which youth can claim for themselves and act upon, where their capacity could be built to provide them with skills to understand themselves and act accordingly in their interaction with the external world. It is a journey from 'self to society'. *Pravah* has developed a curriculum for training for creating the fifth space. The study recognises challenges arising from the present social environment in meeting this objective. The most important ones are co-creating the curriculum and understanding needs of adolescent; contextualising methodology suited to cultural norms and creating space for action with courage to face failures.

Navendu Mishra and Gourav Jaiswal describe the activities of *Agrini*, working in Sehore district of Madhya Pradesh, to make the youth aware of and understand values enshrined in the Directive Principles of the Constitution, as well as functioning of various democratic institutions. This is practised in a public school where students, teachers, guardians and the community work together. The school has a students' parliament which elects a cabinet. Students follow democratic election process, from issuing manifestos, filing nominations for various offices, casting votes, to successful candidates taking oath of office.

These efforts attempt to make adolescents responsible to themselves as well as the wider community. The study cites the case of the student parliament discussing the content of a textbook by the National Council of Education Research and Training. It found the book did not do justice to a freedom fighter. The parliament prevailed on the organisation to make suitable changes. The paper suggests that this experience-based education of understanding the Constitution helps adolescents become responsible citizens. It concludes that adolescents should be taught about the Constitution as their responsibility and not as a mandatory topic of their course work.

Monisha Vemavarapu and her colleagues of *Rubaroo*, an NGO based in Hyderabad, documented a programme to encourage youth to come face-to-face with themselves and the realities of the society they live in, as also how it influences them and how do they connect with these realities ('Nurturing Social Change'). The programme aims to make the youth understand 'me as an adolescent—my responsibilities, my role, and my actions'. Youth should raise questions about what is happening around them and strive to change what they consider unacceptable in a realistic manner. The paper suggests that one should understand the ecosystems of adolescents by working with parents, youth, teachers, and communities. The author also emphasises the importance of the fifth space. *Rubaroo* has also developed an innovative programme on inter-faith dialogues from the perspective of citizenship. The idea of active citizenship implies that adolescents would relate to strangers, interact with them, and empathise with them, enlarging in the process the circle of obligations from individual, peers, and family to the community and world. The paper advocates creating volunteering opportunities for adolescents so as to provide them experience in local development. The paper also lists challenges faced by the NGOs working with youth.

The last chapter in the book sums up the conclusions derived from these papers as well by the observations of highly knowledgeable panels of experts on all three topics, and a large number of concerned citizens, including a group of alert and articulate adolescents who participated in the consultation. The recommendations concern actions needed at the government level as well as for civil society institutions working with youth, for other stakeholders and, equally importantly, for the youth themselves.

2

Education and Citizenship

Abhinav Pandya

India is home to world's fastest and largest growing adolescent population with 35 per cent (358 million) of its population being in the 10–24 age group[1]. In India, policymakers often call this above-mentioned group as our demographic dividend. But, are the adolescents emerging as vibrant, innovative and energetic citizens passionate enough to find solutions for persistent socio-economic, political, and philosophical problems of a society like India, which is going through an eventful phase of transition from a developing into a developed economy?

In this journey to explore ideas to churn out 'good' citizens from our adolescents, first and foremost it becomes essential to find what constitutes a good citizen? Certainly, in today's highly volatile global political scenario where populist nationalism is threatening the civilised global order, an idea of a perfect citizen may veer off into ominous directions adoring the virtues of exclusivist jingoistic nationalism. However, here in this paper, the author intends to find out what a good citizen is in terms of one's responsibility towards society, nation, and the international community in this increasingly globalised world means.

Being a responsible citizen can include diverse areas—legal obligations, social obligations, and moral ones. A citizen has to be law-abiding. But, at times some laws need to be protested against. For example, if a nation has a law prohibiting homosexuality, then the protest against that law may not make one an irresponsible citizen. But, again the methods of protest may be a better judge in such cases. However, broadly speaking, a citizen is expected to be law abiding. But, citizenship is much more than fulfilling one's legal duties. To be a responsible citizen, we should help our communities and those who live in them. So being a responsible citizen encompasses things such as volunteerism, which includes both joining volunteer organisations and performing volunteering work in an individual capacity such as keeping the local parks and lakes clean and helping local businesses. Finally, one has moral obligations. Defining moral obligations is not an easy task. People and societies have different moral codes. However, there are some basics, such as protecting the environment for ourselves and our posterity. There can be no dispute over the question of protecting the environment.

Pravah[2] defines active citizenship as follows:

> 'Citizenship is that, which makes us participative, proactive and responsible towards society. The core values of citizenship include democracy, social justice, equality, peace, respect. Active citizenship refers to the ability of (young) people to be engaged in social action in every walk of life. Where people take ownership for common spaces and act to make change by addressing important social justice issues. This citizenship is boundaryless ... not defined by state, caste, religion, language.'

Presentation by Meenu Venkateswaran, CEO,
Pravah at Nurturing Active Citizenship
among Youth in India: A Consultation

Thus, citizenship implies roles and responsibilities in making the rules of the community, assuming roles and responsibilities in common life and values of a community and the ability and act of engaging with others in tasks that aim to promote the overall well-being and prosperity of the community. The above-mentioned analysis is incomplete without digging into our civilisational roots and appreciating the importance of Dhammapada's ideal of compassion and Gita's ideal of duty towards our family, society, country, and the world community. The idea of 'Vasudhaiva Kutumbkam', i.e. accepting the whole world as one's family might serve as a robust bedrock of the idea of a responsible citizen.

Adolescence and Citizenship

After my return from the United States in 2017, I got a chance to volunteer for an educational institution. For me, it was itself a great learning process because, during my stay of 4–5 years in the United States, India's youth and its aspirations had undergone a tremendous change. I am sharing some of my experience through a case study of sorts, which in some way can bring forth the dilemma of the youth at the crossroads of various complex forces of globalisation, expansive social media, rapid technological transformation, changing social mores, and the forces of identity entwined with traditions, religion, caste, and tribe. The insight into the life and longings of the youth in this institution will help understand their aspirations better and challenges that one comes across as an educationist or a policy expert, in transforming them into responsible citizens.

Kadambari Rural Institute (KRI, name changed) is a non-governmental organisation (NGO) founded in pre-independence days with Gandhian vision and a strong sense of idealism and values of pluralism, secularism, democracy, volunteerism, self-sacrifice, and humility. Below is the story of the students' union elections (2017–18) of the institution. The majority of the KRI students come from a rural and tribal background of Southern Rajasthan. Furthermore, a good number hail from the urban and suburban areas.

In my personal interaction, I found the students to be polite and humble. For me, it was an interesting learning to know that how a healthy community living, nature-oriented lifestyle based on Ayurveda, traditional Indian spiritual systems, rural social structures with roots in joint family, and a deeply entrenched spiritual outlook generates an individual with amazing depth of understanding of the human relations, social norms, and values. As compared with youth from India's metro cities or urban areas, they had a certain ease in gelling with their social environs and adjusting with the older generation. Their understanding, concern, and the bond of mutual existence with the environment was remarkable.

During elections, KRI is quite different from its usual self. Caste, religion, economic strength, and political clout seemed more or less the deciding factors in the elections. The acquisition of power is seen as the ultimate objective. For last many years, local young men of the upper caste and other backward classes had dominated the election outcomes. They had terrorised, threatened, and even beat the other group, i.e. tribal and rural students from Vagad (Dungarpur and Banswara) area into submission. Whoever dared to stand against them was initially offered a monetary incentive to withdraw and if they still persisted they would be threatened and finally roughed up. Their years of experience in student elections made them look like the successors of our mainstream politicians resorting to bribery, caste mobilisation, terrorising, communal sentiments, and muscle power in settling the election scores.

In this year's election also no one was willing to stand against the locals. With great difficulty and assurances of security, I could convince a tribal candidate Sunil Raut (name changed) to stand for the elections. Sunil Raut then made the core team who would occupy key positions, but his core team had all the members from his tribal community, keeping all the upper caste candidates on the fringe. Although he had reservations against the upper caste candidates, I convinced him with strong reasons such as he had no chance of winning the elections without projecting himself as the representative of all the communities. Sunil also had a firm faith in the tactics used by his opponent group but I motivated him to campaign on a strong agenda and concrete plans. I helped him devise election strategy. He went class-to-class for campaigning. The opponent group never had any faith in such democratic methods so they were least bothered with the election campaign of Sunil Raut.

The Election Day saw the college turn into a cantonment with a huge police presence. Lyngdoh committee rules were being flouted openly. Even some lecturers were in cahoots with the criminal elements facilitating the flawed democracy through vote rigging. But to our surprise, Sunil Raut won the elections.

His victory was never accepted by the opposition. He was attacked twice with swords and knives. For days on end, he could not enter the city. Cases were filed by both the parties against each other. Sunil approached the Scheduled Tribes' Commission and the Human Rights Commission. Even after all kinds of persuasion, the student cabinet could not be sworn-in and Sunil had to be content with his name as a president only on the official documents. While all this was happening, the lecturers were happy about the fact that classes were suspended and they had all the free time.

While we are talking about transforming our adolescents into responsible citizens, it becomes essential to talk about our education system. Precisely, this is the reason why I narrated the above-mentioned story. This is not a unique story. The situation and actors detailed above is representative of colleges and universities across the length and breadth of the country in our states. Interestingly, I found most of the actors and students discussed above quite active on social media platforms such as Facebook, Twitter, and Instagram. But, along with the sweeping globalising forces such as internet and social media, they are also deeply entrenched in traditional systems and identities such as caste, tribe, and religion. When it came to communal issues such as Babri Masjid and the murder of Pahlu Khan and Akhlaq over beef eating, most of them found nothing unusual about it. A rumour of beef-consumption is enough to numb the vestiges of their rationality. Reluctantly, they did oppose the killings, but they made it clear that the trajectory of thoughts they pursued in the said matter more or less bordered on rigidity, irrationality, and fanaticism.

For this essay, I interviewed Ajay Singh Mehta. He has a brilliant career in development sector spanning over decades. Currently, he serves as the President of Vidya Bhawan Society, a pre-independence NGO working in the field of education. Ajay sahab feels that as a society we have failed in treating our rural students from the poor socio-economic background with respect. The system has created excellent public schools for students from affluent families for whom quality education is a ticket to the United States and Europe. Further, he argued that when as a society we fail to provide good education and treat the rural students with respect, they become frustrated as there are no jobs for them. It is this frustration that leads them to join lumpen elements or bad student politics or the channels where one's only aim is to seek brute power or money by hook or crook.

Coming to the current happenings in the country, he said that a good citizen in India has to be tolerant and respectful towards minority communities as this attitude has always been there and it has nurtured and sustained the mosaic of India's cultural harmony. Therefore, any exercise or initiative for making a good citizen must focus on the idea of pluralism and respect for diversity.

As the wave of populist nationalism sweeps the world community, the forces of globalisation are in disrepute. At its core, one might want to consider it as a quest for searching and firmly placing oneself in its roots. But, unfortunately, psychological dynamics might just be confined to addressing the fears and insecurities of a mankind in the fast-moving world, but the politics of fear psychosis gets out of control. Norms of citizenship are being redefined, and one can see the phasing away of the values of internationalism from the definitions of a good citizen. In my interview with Kothari, a very senior member of a right-wing nationalist organisation of India, he opined that the youth must have absolute dedication and love for its country, culture, spiritual traditions, and roots. India has suffered enough at the hands of foreign agencies, be it countries, colonial powers, proxies of Pakistan, foreign-funded NGOs, and missionaries engaged in religious conversions. But, now it is time we made our youth aware of these silent and subtle attacks on our cultural roots, and they must be ready to fight this battle tooth and nail in all the domains, i.e. intellectual as well as military.

On the contrary, Suraj Jacob has other worrying concerns about the attributes of a good citizenship in these changing times. He has years of experience in research, teaching, and development in the United States and India. His passion in the field of education inspires him to think of several measures for nurturing responsible citizens. He said that we must train our adolescents in public reasoning. There must be a culture of debate on controversial issues.

Further, Suraj feels that the adolescents must be made aware of one's positionality. We have a tendency to nurture hatred for contrary opinions and lifestyle. He feels that this is because we do not try to see things from other's perspective. If one is aware of his/her or anyone else's existential position in the society, he or she will be able to understand and appreciate other's beliefs and lifestyle in a better and sensible way.

The awareness of one's positionality enables us to understand and accept differences. For example, a Christian born and brought up in India will have a different outlook while looking at the killing of missionaries and beef killings than a New York Times reporter who has never visited India. This is the reason why our youth must be given sufficient academic and cultural exposure to the diversity of not just India but the world community. Further, he preferred Tagore's sense of enlightened nationalism for our youth citizens. He believed that the adolescents must be made aware of the perils of jingoism and must be trained to think in terms of enlightened self-interest.

Having explored the nuances of our adolescents, now it becomes essential to explore the question of what needs to be done to transform them into socially useful and responsible citizens. Personally, I have always felt that in a society like India, education is a very powerful tool to nurture good citizens. In my personal observations and interviews with experienced educationists, I found that our education system lacks the spirit of inquiry. One finds a pitiful absence of critical reasoning, questioning, and argumentation among the students and faculty both, in a country where 'shastratha' is an age-old tradition in metaphysics and spiritual discourse. The existing system hardly fosters any innovation and generates a rigid and a closed mindset.

The teachers want to pour whatever they know, right or wrong, and the students are like jugs. The entire education is based on the paradigm of preaching. If a school cannot produce engineers, chartered accountants, or students smart enough to qualify IAS, then it has no demand. Education is seen as a tool for acquiring power and money. It is not seen as an end in itself. And, with this system, we can produce technocrats and bureaucrats, but we can never produce great writers, scientists, thinkers, philosophers, and visionary public leaders.

Eishita is a young intern exploring the meanings of life at Vidya Bhawan Sansthan, working with its wellness centre. She is a US citizen of Indian origin. Searching for her roots since her childhood often brought her back to India for short visits, which were mostly confined to Mumbai, but she always wanted to explore the real India. Finally, she came to Udaipur for an internship with Sewa Mandir, one of the most prestigious NGOs in rural development in India. Before this interview, she spent a few months in Kotra and Delwara working with the youth including young girls. Life presented a very different picture in Kotra, one of the remotest places in Rajasthan, where the tribal community still practices customs such as blood money or 'mautana'. She says, 'well, the journey is complete now—from New York City to Kotra—it has been a soul-searching experience'.

Eishita feels very passionately for the adolescents of India who are actually at the crossroads between the values of their elder generation that still seep deeply into casteism, tribalism, and ritualistic identities and their rebellious mental urges questioning the meanings of the age-old bondages and knocking the doors of individualism and freedom.

'Well, to make them good citizens, they must have a good sense of confidence in themselves, and for that, they need good mental, physical, emotional, and spiritual health. You give to your community or country what you have. If you are happy, you send happiness; if you are frustrated and confused, you give social and individual chaos and anarchy', observed Eishita with her eyes laden with deep thoughts and the feeling of empathy. She feels that in a diverse country like India, a good citizen must be able to understand people at the deeper level in terms of their social and cultural circumstances. She feels that deeper understanding enables us to understand and manage our frictions better and evolve as a team, as a community and country.

Sharing her experience with the young girls of Delwara village, she said, 'most of them were eager to learn dance and English. Their deep-rooted innocence and happiness could be seen on their faces sparkling with joy. Whereas the girls in cities like Udaipur are more depressed. Girls in Delwara are now breaking out of the shackles of their social system and boldly say that they won't marry before they are 22–23. I motivated them to learn English and dance, which they did, but when I encouraged them to use their English skills to get a job at a local five-star hotel, they did not cooperate. Their parents did not like it. I found it a bit depressing', said Eishita with a tinge of gloom.

Further, she said that the young girls and boys of India need their sexual freedom. This culture of sexual repression is making them mentally distorted and creating a big barrier in their evolution as good citizens with creativity, courage, clarity of thoughts, and high motivation levels. 'I don't understand why young girls of 15 years are compelled to say boys of their age in schools as Bhaiya. Is it the only relation they should know? If they want to explore physical intimacy and love with them ... let them ... what's wrong about it? Such an exploration is the part of one's journey of coming up as a responsible citizen. These boys should know how to talk to girls and give them respect. When you segregate the genders and inject a mindset leading to sexual perversion you are actually facilitating the objectification of women', observed Eishita, with a bit of rebelliousness.

'These adolescents must be given proper sex education. The discussions should not just be about teaching the biological basics. The concepts such as "urge", "consent" and the psychological aspects of sex education must be discussed with them. These are the most important concerns that we must address as a society if we want a healthy and creative mindset', observed Eishita.

Finally, she observed that we have to give respect to the adolescents and their curiosities. Many times, the elders and teachers talk to them in a very insulting tone. If they do not get enough respect for their thoughts and creativity, it will be suppressed right at the outset, and such youth is nothing more than an under-confident, nervous, and lazy bunch or robots.

Pragya Tank is a 24-year-old fellow with an NGO working in the field of education. She has worked as a fellow with Teach for India (TFI) in Ahmedabad. She herself comes from a moderately conservative background of Udaipur. When her friends, cousins, and classmates were sitting for engineering, medical, and MBA exams, she chose an unconventional career track and joined TFI. It was a good deal of struggle as women in her family were born and brought up in a protective environment, but she was going to live with the socio-economically backward Chhara community, famous for their association with petty crime and murder, in Ahmedabad. Narrating her experiences with Chhara community, she said that Chharas are known to be making a livelihood through murder and crime. In 2000, some Chhara families got educated and some of them became lawyers. Since then, they have realised that education is the only way for upward economic mobility, and they are inspiring and motivating their children to get educated.

For them, it is an emotional issue as education is the only way to get prestige and secure a respectable existence for their posterity in a society that still looks at them as murderers and criminals. She also told about the theatre group that Chharas formed and used for social reforms in their community. One of their community members even went to the United States and came back with a Canadian friend who wanted to volunteer for the theatre group, but the police did not allow his friend to work for Chharas. Our legal, social, and political system still looks at

Chharas and communities like them through the colonial lens and perceives them as criminals. Many such tribes were categorised as criminal tribes by British to suit their colonial and political ends, but its time now that we come out of that mindset and respect our people.

'I got huge respect and love from them. Since I was teaching their kids and motivating them to study and make a good life, I was always held in high esteem by them. I never got robbed or molested in their locality and had no issues hanging out with them. And, in fact, I found that with education and right mindset we can make those Chhara adolescents into good citizens whose older generation had made their living by crime. Even now many parents were involved in crime and generally, you would encounter an uncomfortable silence over these matters in the family and Chhara social gatherings. I felt that criminal activities as a mode of living were falling out of fashion and even brought opprobrium in the community. And, it was through education that Chharas wanted to make their adolescents into good citizens', observed Pragya with a very strong sense of hope and insight.

Pragya also narrated the story of a girl who survived the 2002 riots. Neha was living in Kubernagar, Ahmedabad. She registered herself as Neha Bajrangi, but one day Pragya asked her in a casual conversation if she is a Muslim. She got jittery and next day her grandmother requested Neha to not talk about it in public. Neha's family had converted to Hinduism to escape the wrath of Hindu extremists in 2002 Gujarat riots. Her grandmother sold liquor so she got prior warnings and they converted. Pragya told that her grandmother was not much worried about religious matters. Even as Muslims they were following a syncretic religion, which was more or less a mixture of Hindu and Islamic practices. She is scared of the communalisation of society. She just wants peace and does not want any of her family members killed in riots. Pragya was surprised to learn that Neha wanted to become an IPS officer. She was more concerned about the condition of women than Hindu–Muslim politics. 'When she spoke about her father beating her mom, her voice was boiling with rage. She said very confidently that her aim is to stop rapes and domestic violence in society', mentioned Pragya.

Pragya also mentioned a noteworthy phenomenon of destructive westernisation in elite schools. She told that it is like a status symbol to speak in slang-type English, watch English movies, drink, smoke, and do weed. 'These days, girls of class 8th and 9th are having boyfriends not because they are seriously in love or so. It's just because it's a matter of prestige and importance and its cool to have "sex" and boyfriends and then talk about it', said Pragya in a cryptic manner. And, those who cannot have all the above-mentioned things are ridiculed and ultimately get into depression. They suffer from low self-esteem. Because of the inferiority complex, some of them try to cope up by artificially imposing accented English and English movies upon themselves. They also develop distorted notions about love, sexual relations, and women. Artificial lifestyle marked by drugs, alcohol, smoking, affairs, and break-ups ultimately shatters them from within and, instead of national assets, we end up creating youth suffering from depression. And, in this entire matrix of artificiality, they lose their innocence, ideas, originality, and cultural roots. Monetary affluence and a good career become the only sought-after goals.

The Way Out

1. While talking about adolescents and youth, we must keep in mind the differences across the regions and socio-economic divides. The solutions working with the adolescents living in rural areas will have to be different from those applicable for adolescents and youth in urban areas. Even in urban areas, the solutions for elite sections will be different from those for the lower-income groups. For example, a tribal boy can be a good citizen without studying the Second World War. His sociocultural background is more intimate with nature's bounties. So, if he is made aware of ecological concerns and motivated to conserve nature and the traditional knowledge of his tribal community, then also he can become a good citizen. Instead

of bringing the huge population of tribal youth in the formal education system of the country and adding to the army of educated-unemployed, the system must ensure to protect and preserve their natural habitat and social systems.

2. Second, I believe that sound mental, physical, spiritual, emotional, and intellectual potential and health of our youth needs to be explored and developed if we want great scientists, innovators, and philosophers in our country. All the issues of youth that I highlighted in several interviews and case studies made me realise that somewhere our youth at the very basic level is suffering from the following disorders. And, to be precise, the disorders that I am mentioning below are not just confined to youth but to all of us because we have all grown up as adolescents and youth in the same sociocultural milieu: (a) lack of willingness/desire for thinking, questioning, and critical reasoning and (b) lack of sufficient skills/tools that facilitate logical thinking/critical reasoning.

   As a result, most of them do not know what they are doing, why they are doing and what will it lead to. The above-mentioned two traits are the core of the problem. But they lead to several other traits injecting the malfunctioning in young minds such as lack of motivation, self-discipline, positive attitude, determination, interest and rational approach. To fix these ills, the change has to begin with our education system. Since the issue is too wide so for this paper, I will confine myself to a very basic suggestion. First and foremost, we have to change our approach towards education. We have to see education as an end in itself rather than a means to secure power, position and money and prestige in society. From class VI onwards, the focus should be on developing the spirit of inquiry and critical reasoning. One way could be teaching western philosophy, to begin with. Then from class IX, Indian philosophy should be taught. Along with these two, socio-political philosophy and the philosophy of religion should also be taught.

The manner of teaching is very crucial here. First, the core idea should be taught and then it must be related to one's sociocultural and political milieu through stories, anecdotes, and assumption-based situations. Impregnating young minds with the Descartes method of doubt, ideas of Kant, Hegel, Aristotle, syllogism of Nyaya, philosophy of Buddha and Vedanta, Gandhi, Marx, and Humanism will indeed churn their thought process from within and develop the spirit of critical inquiry, creation, and innovation. This novelty should start from the school and continue until the end of their bachelor's programme. Teaching Indian philosophy after western philosophy will enable the flourishing of a good balance of faith and reason as the two cognitive faculties of mankind. Besides this, the youth should also be trained in yoga and meditation, which will develop good physical health and the faculty of intuition. Furthermore, this programme will generate mental aptitude for logical/rational thinking taking a holistic view of things. And, it will develop a scientific temperament for life, relations, nature, society, world, and the universe. Such an approach is the base for learning sciences, literature, politics, humanities, economics, social service, administration, or for that matter handling any field of life. With the above-mentioned programme, I am suggesting training and developing minds in the right directions. With this, the changes in other domains will naturally follow. A youth trained in such a manner is less likely to join a terrorist organisation or kill someone for eating beef or indulge in drugs or become a smuggler.

3. Further, the artificial classifications of science, commerce, and arts need to be done away with. Such archaic and old colonial patterns hinder creativity and act as a barrier to free thinking. And, then there is a hidden caste system, which puts science students at the top, commerce at the second level, and the academically worst lot joins arts courses. The students at the lowest rung of this academic caste system suffer from insult and low self-esteem. Multi-disciplinary

coursework on the pattern of western campuses can be developed.

4. Education as an end in itself—Huge population, shortage of jobs, and a quest for financial stability in a society that is already facing a resource crunch and bad governance make fetching a good job the only goal of education. If the academic programme does not help one get a good social status and financial position, then it has no value or prestige. In my experience, I hardly found our adolescents opting for liberal arts, philosophy, and pure sciences. The young boys and girls face the pressure of passing IIT/PMT or other entrance exams for professional courses. Students of elite schools join good-quality professional programmes either in India or abroad. The middle-class background students in two-tier towns or small towns either try to clear government entrance exams or join some private college through donations. Seeking a good career is not a bad idea. But, we go a step further in the rat race. Most of the private colleges and universities are generating extremely poor-quality doctors and engineers. It is a money-making racket. I have come across universities awarding 980 PhDs in Udaipur. Even the government-run professional programmes are not of a very high academic quality. The research work is extremely poor, and the entire emphasis is on rote learning, and objective is to get a good job and nothing beyond it. Further, the short-cut approach of fetching fake professional degrees is making our youth coward, lazy, vulnerable, and mentally weak. It is killing their motivation and depriving them of any genuine passion or dedication towards the subject. In such a scenario, one cannot think of our education system producing scientists, innovators, public leaders, writers, and philosophers. Therefore, we need a cultural transformation in our education system where education is perceived as an end in itself, not as a means to some other end.

5. Value-based education—Further, we need to promote value-based education. Volunteerism, truthfulness,

discipline, fraternity, respect for diversity, respect for manual labour, sincerity, honesty, commitment, patience, dedication, and perseverance are some values that no doubt make a great human being and a great citizen. I have come across adolescents and youth from the elite schools and colleges of India who are academically very bright and focussed. Professionally, they become successful. But they lacked a sense of idealism. Many of them scoffed at people who spoke in Hindi and openly derided India's cultural, religious, linguistic, and philosophical roots. The curriculum, teaching methodology, and the overall academic culture must impart values, subject expertise (technical and academic), and skills in a harmonious balance. The students must be exposed to nature, forests, wildlife, and community work. If they are taught basic skills in schools such as carpentry, ploughing a field, and shoe making, it will go a long way in developing a respect for manual labour and in general enhance their creativity.

6. The quality of life, i.e. the quality of the air they breathe, the water they drink, and the food they eat, determines the quality of the citizenship of our adolescents. In traditional Indian wisdom, the adage goes that 'Jaisa Khaye anna, vaisa hoye man', i.e. the quality of mind depends on the quality of one's food. Venturing beyond its literal meanings, it conveys deep ecological concerns of our mankind. If we provide a healthy and pollution-free environment, our youth will have a healthy body and mind. And, by healthy, I also mean healthy politics, healthy social norms and values, healthy government (corruption-free), quality public goods, and quality academic institutions. One finds a large number of youth migrating to metro cities for education and jobs. Most of the adolescents from public schools in small towns such as Udaipur, Jhansi, and Indore migrate to metro cities for bachelors, masters, and then jobs. The quality of life in metro cities is pathetic as compared with small cities. Not only do they get dislocated from their roots in small towns and villages but they also get tired, sick, depressed, and frustrated in the fast-paced alien environment of big cities. I

believe that if we provide quality education in colleges and universities in small cities and even villages, the migration will stop and they will have a much better, satisfying, and peaceful life. A peaceful and satisfying life is the key to creativity.

7. Fear-driven education system must end. The exams at the end of the year kill the joy of learning, and the pressure that builds up before the exams terrifies and scares the students. The existing assessment and exam system tests the rote-learning skills, not the analytical skills and their creativity. The assessment systems that go round the year and do not put psychological pressure on students have to be brought in. And, along with that, it should stimulate the interest in the subject and enhance the motivation levels.
8. Further, we need to respect the adolescents and youth as individual human beings with their thoughts, ideas, abilities, and understanding. Ill-treating and insulting their curiosity, choices, ideas, and lifestyle generates inferiority complex. They should be engaged in a respectful dialogue, and that is the only sensible way to enter their minds. Further, the sexual emancipation and sexual empowerment of our youth is also a must for their development. Elders must respect their sexual instincts and choices. Young boys and girls can be seen hiding in jungles for meeting each other and to escape the surveillance of their parents and relatives. Elders have to understand that it is an age where sexual attraction is a natural phenomenon. It cannot be suppressed by artificial, perverted, and unnatural restrictions. Such restrictions will make them frustrated, chauvinist, and perverted. And, it hampers their work efficiency and creativity. Sexual evolution has to take place in a healthy manner. For which, sex education is very essential. Sex education is not just about biology. It should be explored at the psychological and philosophical aspects of a healthy relationship. And, it needs to be mentioned that spiritually, emotionally, intellectually, and physically healthy youth will form healthy relations, which will make them better citizens.

9. To make better citizens, India needs to invest in her mothers and teachers. Currently, the academic standards and ideological vision of the teachers in colleges and schools are extremely poor. While sitting in the interviews for recruiting teachers for class XI and XII of a reputed school in Udaipur, I found that the majority of the candidates had fake BEd degrees, which they got from Bhopal, Kashmir, and several other places. People with a master's degree in economics could not explain the basics of indifference curve, marginal cost, and variable cost. And, the condition of the college teachers was no better. A PhD holder in English could not name any contemporary English author and he had not read a single book after his doctorate. A Political Science doctorate had no idea of thinkers such as Francis Fukuyama. He could not explain the meaning of 'Brexit' to me.
10. Last but not the least, the student politics in colleges needs to be regulated as it is the nursery imparting primary lessons in corruption, casteism, communalism, political kidnappings, and use of muscle and money power. The colleges need healthy and constructive politics, but given the present circumstances, the goal of healthy politics seems like a distant dream. Hence, in the short term, our policies should focus on improving the quality of education, and if that entails cutting down expenditure on useless college politics, then it must be done.

Notes

1. https://everylifecounts.ndtv.com/understanding-adolescence-in-india-616
2. http://www.pravah.org/content/files/Consultation%20Report%20FINAL.pdf

3

Second Chance

A Case Study of Pratham Programme for Dropouts

Pratham Team

Introduction and Background

Established in 1995, Pratham is one of the largest non-governmental organisations in India that focusses on creating high-quality, low-cost, and replicable interventions to address the gaps in the education system. Since 1995, Pratham has strived to work towards realising its vision of 'every child in school and learning well'. Through its flagship Read India programme, Pratham attempts to address the problems in primary education by mobilising and engaging communities and the government (local, state, and central level). Pratham currently reaches 2.2 million children in more than 25,000 villages spread across 20 states through the Read India programme.

The Second Chance programme is another important initiative taken by Pratham in recent years. This initiative aims to assist dropout students (mainly girls) in rural areas to complete their secondary school examinations while simultaneously providing them with soft skills that will support them in the future.

The Second Chance Programme

In the past 10 years, sustained efforts made by the government have led to significant progress in the availability of school infrastructure, particularly at the elementary level. However, poor quality of education, children's inability to cope with the curriculum, and poor socio-economic status result in a steep drop in the number of students who transition from elementary to secondary school. Pratham's experience as well as different sources of information and research suggest that a combination of many factors are responsible for dropping out of school, including lack of reasonable access to secondary schools, inadequate learning levels and unfavourable social and cultural conditions for education of girls specifically or secondary education in general.

As mentioned above, the Second Chance programme aims to address issues of access to education and learning for students who are in school as well as those who have dropped out. The aim of the programme is two-pronged in nature. At one level, teachers and facilitators at the Second Chance centres find ways to bring back all those who had dropped out of school for a variety of reasons. Two, special focus is given to bring back women/girls who are often prevented from continuing their education owing to gender constraints. This means not only rekindling their and their family's interest in education but also preparing girls adequately in terms of honing their confidence and ability to manage and live a better-quality life.

Hence, the main objectives of the Second Chance programme are as follows:

1. To help primarily girls and women from underprivileged communities to complete their secondary school education;
2. To provide an opportunity to study along with an environment that encourages progress and success; and
3. To focus on personality development and confidence building to empower the girls/women in their daily lives as well as in their studies.

The programme provides academic and personal support needed to enable students to appear for their Secondary School Examination (Grade X). Today the Second Chance programme operates in more than 30 centres across nine states (Andhra Pradesh, Bihar, Chhattisgarh, Gujarat, Madhya Pradesh, Maharashtra, Odisha, Rajasthan, and Telangana) and has reached more than 4,300 students in 2016–17 alone. The programme has also seen a steady increase in the percentage of students passing in their final board examination. In 2012–13, the pass percentage was approximately 51 per cent; by 2013–14, this had jumped to 67 per cent; and the results of 2015–16 showed a further increase to 88 per cent of enrolled students successfully clearing their final board examinations.

Course Overview

The programme is divided into three phases. In the first phase, faculty members and tutors are trained by the National Curriculum team. Faculty members and tutors are also involved in the mobilisation process, which involves identifying locations where there are school dropouts, spreading awareness about the Second Chance programme in these areas, and speaking to potential students and their parents about the programme and encouraging them to enrol into the Second Chance programme. Potential candidates for the Second Chance programme include girls who have not completed their secondary schooling and have a gap of a minimum of two years. However, Pratham encourages anyone to enrol, regardless of class and year of drop out, if they have some level of basic reading and numeracy skills.

In the second phase, after the students join the Second Chance programme, they are enrolled into a 3–4-month Foundation Course (FC), which is aimed at bridging the gap between basic concepts and the secondary school curriculum. The FC is aimed at strengthening basic knowledge of students and also to prepare them for the Main Course (MC). In the beginning, a simple assessment is used to understand the level of individual children and of the group to categorise them according to learning levels for instruction. After the first month of FC, a pre-test is conducted to understand the learning levels of students. Their growth is tracked over the next 3–4 months. At the end of the FC, students are evaluated on the basis of an internal examination. Based on their performance in the exam, their motivation, and regularity in attendance, students move to the third and last phase of the programme, which is the MC in which Grade X curriculum is taught.

Table 1 highlights the important events that take place in an academic year. While there will be slight differences in the state academic calendars, Table 1 is a prototype of one such calendar.

Table 1

Activity Calendar

Month	*Activities*
April	Foundation Course training for faculty and tutors by National Curriculum team
April–May	Mobilisation and recruitment of students by Pratham
May–September	Foundation Course
September	Main Course training for faculty and tutors by National Curriculum team
September–April	Main Course
December–January	Mock tests
April	State board exam
June	X class examination results

Course Content and Curriculum

As mentioned previously, the main focus of the Second Chance programme is to prepare students for the board examination within a time frame of approximately 12 months. To achieve these ambitious objectives, the course is divided into two sections: a 3–4-month FC and a 6-month MC.

The FC involves classes in Maths, Language (e.g. Hindi, Gujarati, Marathi, Telugu, and Urdu depending on the state), English, and Science/Home Science as applicable, while the MC tackles the demanding Grade X curriculum. Subjects offered in the MC vary across states, as does the medium of instruction as it depends on the options available in the relevant examination board. A typical set of courses might include Hindi or the state language, Maths, English, Science/Home Science, Social Science, Computer Literacy, and other elective courses.

In addition to the course content for Grade X exams, Pratham also runs modules on life skills for students to prepare themselves for situations that they are likely to come across in their lives and builds their confidence in dealing with these situations. Additionally, training in 'soft skills' is a component that runs across both course modules. While the focus is on academic preparation, soft skills training is intended to enhance students' employability. Besides life skills, which are carried out during the FC, Pratham also offers supplementary courses such as Health and Hygiene and Nutrition based on Early Child development programmes.

An important aspect of the Second Chance programme is that the focus is largely on giving confidence to students, in addition to completing the prescribed curriculum. Pratham's experience of working with children who drop out of school at various stages has been kept in mind while designing the course. Another aspect that is taken into consideration when designing the course curriculum is that most students who enrol for the programme can devote very limited time for assignments/studies. As a result, the course is mainly centred on classroom-based activities and assignments.

Further, there is a wide variation in exams across different states. While in some states, students appear for the state board exams, in other states, they opt for National Institute of Open Schooling (NIOS). Therefore, to deal with different board syllabus, the content team usually goes through the Grade X curriculum of different states and topics are selected for each module, which may vary according to state board requirements. More focus is given to the topics that have more weightage in the board exams and are simple to understand. During the first year, each participating state chooses the medium for appearing for the Secondary Exams. In some cases, these choices have evolved over time and Second Chance centres in several states are now affiliated with India's National Institute of Open Schooling (NIOS).

Implementation Model

The Second Chance programme is being implemented via centres. Currently, there are about 30 centres, and each centre caters to approximately 100 candidates who are spread across 25–75 villages in rural areas and 2,000–3,000 households in urban areas. There are mainly three delivery models that are being followed in different states.

Residential Hub Model

The model is typically structured as a central hub with four to five linked spokes. The central teaching hub caters to students from three to five cluster centres set up in the region. Each cluster centre enrols a group of 10–20 girls from nearby villages. Each cluster has a tutor who guides the students in their daily studying, assists them with take-home worksheets, and addresses issues in all subjects. For 20 days a month, they work with a tutor at their cluster centre, and for five days a month, girls from all cluster centres travel to the teaching hub where they live and attend focussed classes with Second Chance faculty members.

Non-Residential Hub Model

The Non-Residential Hub model operates along the same pattern as the Residential Hub model, except that instead of living at the hub centre for five days each month, students commute from their homes. In contexts where commuting is not an issue for the girls, this makes it easier for families to allow their daughters to attend classes.

Roving Model

In this model, students do not have to travel beyond their local cluster centre; instead, faculty members rotate through a set of five cluster centres in the area and spend 5 days a month at each centre before moving to the next. This model is particularly useful in the more rural locations where it can be difficult to find individuals with the qualifications required to become tutors in the cluster centres. In 2014–15, Madhya Pradesh, Maharashtra, and Andhra Pradesh adopted this model.

Second Chance in Patna, Bihar offers a different model of support to girls in the slum communities of urban Bihar and for girls who are 14 years and above. The centres in Bihar conduct classes for two years. There are four centres in Patna, also known as Community Learning Centres, and girls from the neighbourhood communities attend classes at the centre for 5–6 hours every day. Going forward, from 2017 to 2018 the model will change to one-year Roving Model.

In 2016–17, except for Chhattisgarh and Odisha, which still follow the Residential Hub centre model, other states are following the Non-Residential or Roving Models. In each case, an average of five cluster centres is set up in each selected block.

Faculty and Tutors

Second Chance centres are run by full-time Pratham staff. At the state level, the team includes a Second Chance coordinator and a State Resource Group (SRG), which comprises four subject specialists (one each for Maths, Language, English, and Life Skills/Science/Home Science). Along with annual trainings, one of the main roles of SRGs is to provide on-going support to faculty and tutors through demonstrations of teaching methods, exam-oriented preparation, and content creation. As they spend nearly 2–3 weeks each month visiting different centres, SRGs are able to regularly monitor the functioning of various centres. A central programme team is also in place to support state- and centre-level personnel in the areas of content development, programme management, and administration.

Each Second Chance centre has one centre incharge, four faculty members, and five tutors. While faculty members are subject specialists and typically rotate across cluster centres and help students with new concepts or lessons, tutors are responsible for working with and supporting the students on a day-to-day basis.

Recruitment for each centre is done locally, on the basis of experience and background, in education studies. Along with a bachelor's degree coupled with BEd, MEd, or DEd, applicants (for both tutors and faculty) are also evaluated on their conceptual clarity in basic maths, communication, and writing skills. Furthermore, qualities such as willingness to learn new methods of teaching, passion for working at grass-roots level, ability to mobilise, and their connect with students are also taken into consideration when choosing the right applicants. Recruitment of faculty and tutor is based on written test and teaching demo followed by interview.

The academic teams are given extensive training in curriculum and pedagogy on a regular basis. The role of the faculty and tutor is more of a facilitator, and therefore, huge emphasis is given on this during the training. In the Second Chance programme, faculty training takes place twice a year. First training is organised at the beginning of the FC, and the second training is organised at the beginning of the MC. Main course training covers course content that is relevant for board examination. The Central Resource Group trains state-level trainers, who in turn conduct training for faculty and tutors. Continuous support through visits and calls is provided to the state teams throughout the year. Refresher trainings are planned on the basis of inputs and feedback received from the state teams. In addition, a month-wise calendar is prepared to ensure that the course is completed in a time-bound manner. Careful planning is needed to ensure that each topic is taught by the faculty and then reinforced by the tutors, and students' understanding is carefully assessed via regular assignments and mock tests.

Faculty and tutors play a large role in the Second Chance programme. To keep the students engaged in learning, the content team regularly visits different clusters and interacts with SRGs to understand the challenges being faced by the team. They also interact with students to understand the issues they face during the learning process. This regular interaction helps the content team in improving the teaching material and learning process.

Teaching-Learning Methods

Over the past 20 years, Pratham has worked to strengthen children's foundational learning. In the process, the organisation has developed its own teaching–learning package known as Combined Activities for Maximised Learning (CAMaL). Core principles of the CAMaL approach include focussing on a specific target group of children, articulating clear learning goals, using appropriate teaching–learning activities and materials, and organising children into groups on the basis of their ability level. Underlying the entire process, on-going simple measurement of children's ability to read, write, comprehend, and do basic arithmetic and solve problems is used to assess progress.

In CAMaL methodology, teaching–learning activities include whole class participation, group activities, and individual tasks such as reading and writing. For students who are in the early stages of learning, more emphasis is given on listening and speaking in the group. As they move up to higher levels of learning, individual reading and writing activities become more important. Shorter texts prepared from the Class X syllabus are incorporated in the activities of the FC, which follows the CAMaL methodology as it helps students to grasp various topics faster.

Along with various innovative teaching methods, Digital Content was introduced in 2015–16. As a part of the pilot, computers were installed in three blocks of Maharashtra—Satara, Solapur, and Nagpur. Science and Maths content was introduced through videos in the Pratham Open School application, TATA Class Edge software, and YouTube videos.

Student Assessment

Two main assessments are carried out at Second Chance centres.

Internal Assessments

When learners join the Second Chance programme, an internal assessment is done to evaluate their learning levels. After the completion of FC, tests are again carried out for the subjects that have been taught and pre- and post-test scores[1] are compared to help the facilitators assess the learning improvement of students and their preparedness to take up Grade 10 curriculum. While the final assessment remains the board examinations, which determines the success of the programme, each state conducts mock tests (two to three per state), which is based on the relevant board pattern. Along with the mock tests, centres also regularly give monthly exams, worksheets for practice, and previous years' exam papers to help students prepare for the board exams.

External Assessment

ASER Centre has recently mapped all contents of the FC and is creating additional tools based on this framework, which will be used as external assessments for the students. This assessment is competency based and will allow the Second Chance programme National Content team to certify the students if they clear the FC. Pratham is also working towards creating assessments for some basic vocational skills and life skills.

A Management Information System (MIS) is used to track, record, and monitor different aspects of student information and analyse how they affect student performance in the final exam. For example, some of the things that are tracked include learner's level at pre-test, improvements made in post-test, competencies in Maths have been achieved and yet to be achieved, learners' performance in pre-board and mock tests. For the programme, MIS also gives reports on how many students were enrolled, how many have dropped out, how many have registered for their exams, etc. The MIS is also used to track student performance in internal assessments and the final board exams.

Foundation and Main Courses

The content and modules for the Second Chance programme are designed to suit the needs of students who enrol for the programme, and the content has evolved over the past five years.

Although the content of the modules was initially focussed on preparing students for Grade X examination, the programme has evolved over the years, and several modifications have been made so that the content now goes beyond the academic curriculum.

Foundation Course

Students who join the Second Chance programme are not regular school-going students. Most of them have been out of the school system for many years. Because of this, students' mastery of basic skills, their knowledge and understanding of academic content, and their level of self-confidence are often quite limited.

Accordingly, the FC is a 3–4 month 'bridging' course intended to help students regain study habits and master foundational skills, so as to prepare them to face the demanding Grade X curriculum. In addition, the FC provides students with key life skills such as public speaking, critical thinking, decision-making, and teamwork that are important regardless of whether students continue on to the MC. The first month of the FC focusses on developing basic reading and mathematical competencies of students. Here, the focus is on building foundational skills. After that, they move to Advance FC, where other modules are introduced.

The main objective of the FC is to help students reach a level where they can understand the main course syllabus of Class X. For this purpose, the FC starts by covering the very basic level of Mathematics. The aim is to achieve basic understanding of numbers, operations, and mathematical keywords. Basic FC covers number recognition, addition and subtraction, and multiplication and division. After the completion of Basic FC, there is a test, and students who pass the test move on to

Advance FC, which includes topics such as Arithmetic, Algebra, Basic Geometry, and Measurements.

In the Language foundation course, students are made to understand letters, words, and sentences in a manner so that they are able to read and write fluently. The basic purpose of the foundation course is to help students practice language skills on a regular basis, as passing class X examinations depends on the writing ability of the students.

In Science, the FC starts by covering the very basic concepts of Science. The aim is to introduce Science vocabulary and basic understanding of concepts in Physics, Chemistry, and Biology. Another objective is to familiarise students with different methods of learning Science.

In English the Foundation course is subdivided into three modules:

1. Reading and writing readiness including learning new vocabulary;
2. Syntax and sentence comprehension;
3. Introduction to grammar and reading paragraphs/stories;

Whereas in Home Science, the topics not only include the basics of health issues, different diseases, nutrition, and child care, it also opens up opportunities in the field of fashion and food industry, interior decoration, and health and nutrition.

Apart from core subjects, the Life Skills module runs during the FC of the Second Chance programme. This is to promote mental well-being and that lead to a healthy and productive life. Life skills develop competencies that result in behaviours that lead to personal growth and positive and meaningful responses to life situations.

The Life Skills module in the Second Chance programme covers first seven out of the 10 life skills listed by the World Health Organization. Some topics/sessions of the module are repeated during the main course. Students of the Second Chance programme have been generally away from formal education for a considerable period of time. Hence, they tend to be shy, less confident, and heavily dependent on their families for life decisions. The Life skills module helps them to open up, think independently, and gain confidence over time. The module equips them with different skills and tools. This helps them take better decisions, plan their personal and professional lives well, thereby building their capacity to deal with immediate as well as future challenges.

Under each subject, students undergo three main evaluations, which help the faculty and tutors to track the performance of the students.

Main Course

The MC is designed to cover Grade X curriculum over a period of six months. As mentioned earlier, different states follow different boards and therefore have different examination patterns. Also, programme implementation varies from state to state. For example, board exams in some states take place before others. Therefore, subjects offered in the MC vary across states, as does the medium of instruction. A typical set of courses includes Hindi or the state language, Maths, English, Science/Home Science, Social Science, Data Entry, and other electives. On an average, each module is designed as a 220-hour intervention. Overall, the main course typically involves four sessions a week of 5–6 hours each for 27 weeks.

Content for the MC is developed on the pattern of state boards. Common topics from different states are selected on the basis of topics that get more weightage in the board exams. To illustrate, topics such as Equation, Triangles, Circle, and Mensuration get more weightage compared with other topics. Therefore, for MC, following topics are usually covered (there are always some variations across each state): Since both Language and Social Science curriculum of Class X is tough, the faculty prepares fact retrieval questions based on each lesson. The summary is written based on answers of fact retrieval questions. Usually the summary is written based on these questions and gives a gist of the lessons that are taught using CAMaL methodology. This helps students who are not comfortable with reading long lessons with difficult vocabulary to attempt to write answers based on these lessons. Additionally, worksheets are prepared based on the pattern of board examination. The main purpose here is to help the students understand the chapters so that they can understand the grammar, read and write on their own, and answer questions.

In English, content for the MC is developed based on the pattern of state boards or NIOS, whichever is applicable in each state. The main objective is to prepare students for the board exams. Therefore, following aspects are covered in the MC:

1. Help students understand the text books through lesson summary;
2. Facilitate learning through peer learning and working in small groups;
3. Familiarise students to the exam pattern;
4. Help them to prioritise the questions that should be attempted first; and
5. Help them to complete the paper in the given time limit.

Also, during the course, the focus is given more on topics in which students can get high score with minimum efforts. These topics include letter writing, report writing, dialogue writing, and story writing.

Apart from core subjects, Computer Applications are also part of the MC in states where this subject is offered under state board/open school examination for Class X. Most students show a lot of interest in this module as most of them never had a chance to work on computers. This module is also important because many students find the module useful for future job opportunities including data entry operators at the local gram panchayat, milk cooperatives, and even as a computer teacher in the local primary schools. For example, in Maharashtra, all students who complete Class X exams can study computer course, which is certified by the Maharashtra State Certificate in Information Technology. This certificate is a mandatory criterion when they apply for government jobs.

Going Forward

Since its inception, the Second Chance programme has seen a steady increase in both coverage and success. In 2011, the programme reached 390 girls. By 2016–17, this number had increased to 4,330. Similarly, girls' performance in the Grade X board exams has shown enormous improvement over the years. In 2011–12, very few cleared the exams, but three years later, the pass rate was above 80 per cent. In 2015–16, an attempt was made to understand what happens to these students after 12-month intervention is over. In a survey, about 90 per cent students were tracked, and it was found that many learners from the Second Chance programme went on to further studies or paid employment. For example, in Gujarat, the centre incharge was able to link 11 women to a local pharmaceutical manufacturing unit, which provided the women with employment as they had successfully completed their Grade X examinations. These women were happy to have found jobs close to their homes and are now contributing to their household income. In another instance, learners from the Second Chance programme underwent a short course on health and hygiene immediately after their board examination. The visiting resource person, a doctor in the nearby hospital, offered a few of them training for employment as nursing assistants.

More importantly, participation in the Second Chance programmes has given these girls an enormous boost in terms of their self-confidence. Kalpana, a student from Maharashtra, had joined the Second Chance programme in her late twenties in 2014–15. She shared with pride an anecdote about her son's improvement in maths. 'He told his teachers that his mother inspired him by relentlessly struggling to get her lessons right and now he wants to do the same', she said. Education has made her the pride of her household. Similarly, other students in Adhikpur, Odisha explained how she related mathematics with her daily life. Before joining the Second Chance programme, she worked as Asha Tai. When administering polio drops, she had to place the dropper at an angle of 40 degrees. It is only after the completion of the programme that she understood the relevance and the concept behind 40-degree angle.

The Second Chance programme started out as an effort to give school dropouts a second chance at education, but the outcomes of the programme are not limited to number of students successfully passing their board exams. Teachers and students alike mention changes in the personality of the students over the course of the programme and beyond; through lessons on life skills, soft skills, and vocational training, we are enabling our students to explore and create new options in their lives. These personal transformations are an important and valued outcome of the Second Chance programme.

Over the past 5 years, Pratham has had the experience of delivering the Second Chance programme in nine states across the country covering six languages. Given the success of the programme to date, the organisation is in a position to streamline, revise, and repackage the Second Chance programme content, materials, processes, and tools so that they are useable by others. The content also gets regularly updated based on the changes in the state board curriculum. As a result, the content team is constantly engaged in creating course materials and worksheets that are in line with the changes in the curriculum. Past experiences with students also help the team in making the content more robust and user friendly. A lot of focus is given to building the capacity of tutors, and teaching learning strategies keep evolving based on the needs and requirements of the students. The content team is also working on developing materials that can be used for distance learning as an option for students.

Going forward, the Second Chance team is deliberating on sharing its learning for in-school students, improving their learning levels so they are better retained in school and complete their schooling. It also includes educational pathways that can be offered to students beyond academics such as training on vocational courses and ways of enhancing their capacities to cope with life situations.

Note

1. These tests have been developed by ASER Centre.

4

Adolescent Learning and Empowerment Education

Case Study of Doosara Dashak

Shobhita Rajgopal

Introduction

The period of adolescence has been recognised as a period of rapid psychosocial, cognitive, and behavioural maturation. In recent years, the challenges facing adolescents have been analysed and documented extensively. Adolescents are a heterogeneous group with diverse needs that vary depending on factors such as age, gender, marital status, place of residence, and educational attainment. Adolescence is also a time when gender roles diverge sharply. Girls and boys experience adolescence in very different ways.

The role of education as a key driver for both social and economic well-being of adolescents is well recognised. There has been a concerted effort on the part of the governments and development partners to address the needs of young people through policies and programmes directed specifically at them. Despite these efforts, adolescents continue to face a number of vulnerabilities and challenges, highlighting the gaps in the implementation of programmes and policies.

Doosra Dashak (DD; second decade) [1] was initiated in Rajasthan in 2001, by Foundation for Education and Development with the aim of empowering adolescents in the age group of 11–20 years. The focus was on giving a 'second chance' and developing a sense of self-worth among out-of-school adolescents and promoting skills for life to them. The objectives as formulated in the initial proposal included meeting the basic learning needs of adolescents, their health care, imparting vocational and life skills, and utilisation of science and technology to develop and harness the adolescents' energies for nation building (Saldhana 2007: 54–55). The project strategies were based on an understanding that holistic and integrated education was not only about imparting knowledge but also focussed on the development of personality of the adolescent learners, meeting their learning needs, and equipping them with skills for future.

The founder members believed that out-of-school adolescents were, in general, a neglected lot with neither the state nor society giving them due respect and regard. They yearned to live a life of respect and dignity acquired through opportunities for basic education tailored to their needs and circumstances and life skills that would make them useful and productive citizens in the context of the social and cultural milieu of rural Rajasthan (DD Forum Report 2016).

DD was started initially in two blocks, Kishanganj (in Baran) and Bap, (in Jodhpur) in June and July 2001, respectively. Over the past decade and a half, DD has spread to nine blocks across seven districts of Rajasthan, covering 190 villages across 71 panchayats. The intervention areas are diverse in geographic conditions, socio cultural milieu, and community coverage. The implementation of the project, therefore, has taken into account the diversity with strategies tailored to suit local contexts.

The present case study attempts to highlight the genesis, approach, key processes, challenges, and opportunities in addressing multiple needs of out-of-school adolescents in Rajasthan. The case also discusses the enabling factors that have facilitated *DD Sahbhagis* to chart new pathways both at the individual and collective levels.

This case study is divided into two sections—Section I discusses the genesis and early experiences of the project and analyses the key processes and various interventions strategies; and Section II focusses on the gains and challenges emerging from the intervention to inform policy and practice.

Section I

The state of Rajasthan has the distinction of being a state where many innovative educational projects like Women's Development Project, Shiksha Karmi Project, and Lok Jumbish have been implemented. All these programmes had an indirect influence on planning of DD. The early discussions recognised the need to design an educational intervention that would take into account multiple concerns of adolescents who did not have an opportunity of schooling.

Doosra Dashak: Early Beginnings

The need for an intervention like DD was based on the premise that adolescents can play the role of catalysts in the process of social transformation. The proposed vision was 'creation of a new social order through community participation, based on values of equity and justice; providing a second chance for education to the unschooled adolescents and the preparation of a cadre of committed adolescents and young persons equipped with relevant education and skills'.

The specific objectives as elaborated in the project proposal in 2000 were as follows:

1. To meet the basic learning needs of adolescents and to relate learning to their life, work, and environment;
2. To enhance critical awareness so that they understand their present situation and take measures to change it through proactive interventions;

3. To equip them for adolescent and family life through an improvement in their health awareness;
4. To enhance vocational and life skills;
5. To harness their energies for nation building through creation of cadres who would be educated, informed, and responsible leaderships; and
6. To employ science and technology for improving the lives of people. (DD, project proposal to Teacher Eligibility Test (TET), September 2000, as cited in Saldhana 2007: 53)

The holistic approach aimed at leadership and action made the education of adolescents both an 'objective' and a means of empowerment. The project sought to invest in adolescents as an active force for social reconstruction.

The key strategies and processes were based on the understanding that education entails not only imparting knowledge but development of the personality of adolescent learners, meeting their learning needs, and equipping them with information for their future roles. DD entailed working closely with community, building organisations of youth and women, developing a holistic and integrated education framework, developing a system of continuing education, working with local governments, and so on.

DD made its beginnings in two blocks, Kishaganj in Baran District and Bap in Jodhpur in 2001. In 2003, two new blocks were taken up—Bali in Pali district and Abu Road in Sirohi district. In 2005, DD further expanded to Pisangan in Ajmer. At the end of the 4th year of the project, 221 revenue villages in 38 gram panchayats across five districts were covered. These blocks were primarily selected because of their remoteness, poor socio-economic conditions, low education outreach, and presence of marginalised populations like *Sahariyas*, *Garasiyas*, Muslims minority, and scheduled caste (SC) groups who were living in extreme deprivation and seclusion. The existence of some human resource and organisational support was an added criterion.

In 2007, several new blocks were added—Laxmangarh in Alwar, Bassi in Jaipur, Pindwara in Sirohi, and Desuri in Pali district. As of March 2017, DD project is being implemented in nine blocks of seven districts of Rajasthan, covering 190 villages of 71 Panchayats.

Key Strategies and Processes

The DD project strategies and processes have focussed on linking social and ecological environment and experience with learning; such learning in turn is seen to influence thought, behaviour, and practice of learners. Therefore the main activities of the project that have crystallised over time include:

Community Mobilisation and Social Mapping

Community mobilisation and social mapping help lay the foundation of the project in the selected intervention areas. Intensive interaction with community members in the selected villages/gram panchayats, teachers of local non-governmental organisations (NGOs), and block-level government officials help inform them about the project strategies. The discussions and social mapping exercises also lead to understanding the educational needs of adolescents in the area and identifying adolescents for camps.

Residential Camps (Long and Short Duration)

A key strategy to address adolescent needs and capacity building are the residential camps and short-term training camps. The emphasis on residential training sought to inculcate a sense of togetherness among rural adolescents irrespective of caste, class, and religion. Each adolescent who participates in a residential camp or training becomes a DD sahbhagi and continues to receive inputs through his/her adolescent years for building knowledge and values in keeping with DD's vision. DD believes that each sahbhagi should live an enlightened life and engage in civic action to build a better society (Sinha 2013: 9).

In the beginning, no rigorous process of selection of participants was followed, and the process of selection emerged over a period of time. In Kishanganj, girls were selected through a one-week camp. The girls returned to their villages and identified boys who were not enrolled in schools for training. However, in Bap, the selection of girls was extremely difficult, given the social attitudes towards educating girls; so a beginning was made with boys. In subsequent blocks, adolescent girls who had gone through the residential camps took leadership roles and worked with the community. In Abu Road, an effort was also made to work with the Garasia Samaj Sudhar Samiti to further the DD vision and seek support in identifying adolescents for camps.

Residential camps of 4-month duration are organised for out-of-school adolescents thus identified. These camps aim at facilitating teaching and learning, numeracy and literacy skills of Grade 3–5 levels, and confidence building. Generally, separate camps are held for girls and boys. Given that majority of the adolescents have been/are first-generation learners or early dropouts, the camps have had to take into account the varying needs of adolescents. Issues related to safety and securities of girls have also been given priority. A team of dedicated full-time trainers with good academic record conduct the various activities in the residential camps.

Over the years, several camps have been organised in various DD blocks. For many of the adolescents attending the camp, it has been a process of self-discovery. The residential camps have led to minimising of age-old structures of inequity based on class, caste, gender, and religion. Equal importance has also been given to building self-confidence and raising awareness on issues of gender equality health/hygiene, water and sanitation, local governance, and rights.

The project review carried out for the period 2010–13 also notes that:

> The camp provides a nurturing environment for teaching the children. Students valued several features of the camps, such as a structured routine that included space for learning and

> recreation. They also liked the culture of openness and fearlessness and the caring attitude of the teachers. The participation in the camp is central to giving many of them an opportunity to resume their education. The camp has been successful in helping a significant proportion of children join mainstream education. Some of these get admission to the Kasturba residential schools [2] that run from Grades 6 to 8 for girls from marginalised groups living in remote areas. The camps also provide an opportunity for the more talented and skilled *sahbhagis* to take on teaching roles and possibly develop careers in development. Participation in the camp and exposure to DD's values make them want to study and even creates aspiration for taking up jobs such as school teachers. (Sinha 2013: 4)

A more recent review carried out in 2016 also points out that:

> In Bali, about 50 girls who had dropped out or never gone to school, and were taught basic literacy skills in the camps along with other life skills according to the 13 parameters defined by the organisation. Here too the organisation and planning was excellent, as was the general cleanliness, comfort, and cheerful loving atmosphere that were provided. At different times of the day when the camp was visited, activities in the groups were in full swing, and discussions with the girls showed that this was normal routine for them. The records revealed that most girls would be able to achieve a Class 3 literacy level by the end of the camp, with a few, maybe 25 per cent, achieving Class 5 level. (Srinivasan 2016: 10–11)

Over the project period, short-duration camps on specific themes, such as life skills education, have also been organised. Other residential programmes have focussed on livelihood, governance, organisational skills, participatory monitoring, and evaluation and documentation.

An effort has also been made to prepare adolescents to complete their secondary schooling through open and distance learning (ODL). ODL is not new to DD. This concept was first introduced in 2003–04 in Kisahanganj block of Baran district. A residential camp was organised where 38 adolescent girls of age

15 and above were enrolled to prepare for Open Middle School examination. DD continued to encourage adolescents from 2007 to 2012 to take Open School exams by organising special classes for them. As a result, over the years, 5,386 adolescent boys and girls have appeared for open school examinations.

In 2016–17, Bap block initiated an experiment in Open Schooling (OS) for adolescent girls above 14 years of age. A 4-month residential camp was organised for only older adolescents (over the age of 15 years). The decision was not easy; there were many doubts at the beginning pertaining to the choice of curriculum to be used in the camp, capability of 18 teachers to conduct such camps, and so on. The greatest challenge was to motivate and bring older girls to the camp, some of whom were married and had joined the work force. Though the task seemed difficult, the response was very encouraging. In total, 59 girls applied for enrolment and each agreed to contribute ₹ 1,000 for the camp. Finally, on the basis of a benchmark evaluation, 49 adolescent girls and women enrolled in the camp, out of which 42 have applied for open school examination this year (DD Annual Report 2016–17).

Rajagopal and Chakravarthy (2016) in their interaction with girls at the Bap camp for OS found that:

> The Doosra Dashak program in Bap provided girls the opportunity to fast-track their education and prepare for Class 10 examination for open schooling during the course of 4 months. Apart from the educational curriculum, the program also enabled confidence building and life skills. Many girls in the group were vocal and confident, and supported and encouraged by the trainers and project staff; they were confident of avoiding marriage till the age of 18 years. Several girls mentioned that they would like to be as educated as their male partners so they have an equal standing in the relationship. The program being a residential one provides girls the opportunity to live away from their family context' and with their peers, this helps them to meet girls from across villages, exposing them to realities other than their own and to newer opportunities. The programme also teaches girls basic computer skills and promotes cross learning. For instance, one

of the girls in the programme who is very good at stitching was teaching other interested girls the skill—a sewing machine had been arranged for them.

Having undergone the programme for over a month, many of the girls confidently expressed the desire to be educated and employed, stand on their own feet, and not be dependent on anyone. Few girls also said that if educated, they could stand up for themselves and report abuse, if required.

Most of the girls who were enrolled in the camp came from marginalised communities where families are involved in agriculture. A month in the programme had taught girls confident public speaking, ability to negotiate their agency to an extent, and an understanding of issues of gender equality and child marriage. Girls displayed and explained charts and pictorial representations of their daily learning as a part of the programme. They felt that the camp had enabled education for dropout and un-enrolled girls. The programme not only provided examination-oriented learning, but an overall skill building for girls, so they have the ability to address issues that affect their lives beyond the programme as well.

Micro-planning

Work on the micro-planning process was initiated in August 2003, after two years of intensive deliberation. Micro-planning in DD combines the monitoring of participants, reviewing the project outcomes, and planning for the future. Project implementation is seen to be facilitated through sustained contact with participants and assessment of the quality of residential training followed by monitoring at 6-monthly intervals. A benchmark is established at the outset through an understanding of the entry-level skills of the adolescent participant. An assessment of progress is further made at the end of a residential training and later monitored at 6-monthly intervals. The assessments are based on the basis of 13–15 parameters. These include literacy, language, arithmetic, leadership qualities, articulation skills, equality of caste and religion, democracy and democratic values, rural development, personal cleanliness, cleanliness of surroundings, health and nutrition, reproductive health, maternal health, information about health facilities, drinking water, and substance abuse.

The indictors of each parameter are visualised at three levels:

1. acquired knowledge and understanding;
2. its translation into personal life; and
3. willingness of participants to serve others in the community.

A grading of each participant with respect to each parameter bearing in mind the indicators is attempted on a five-point scale from A to E, where A denotes the highest level of performance and E the lowest. Data collected through this process are collated and classified. This serves both as a review and a planning process. The evaluation framework also helps the DD staff to mainstream them in government schools, Kasturba Gandhi Balika Vidyalayas (KGBVs), and tribal hostels.

Ikhvelo Centres

Ikhvelo centres have been set up at the panchayat level to facilitate continuing education and promoting reading and learning amongst the adolescents and youth, who are the beneficiaries of various DD camps and trainings. Over the years, these centres have also emerged as multipurpose centres for community and adolescents.

The Ikhvelos provide the following facilities:

1. Information/Resource Centre—providing information about the various government schemes and how to access them;
2. Open and Distance Learning Centres—providing opportunities to adolescents to prepare for Open School exams, take up short-term courses, and help students attending regular school;
3. Community Science Centre—inculcating scientific temper;
4. Library cum Reading Room; and

5. Cultural and Recreational Centre—providing equipment for sports and recreation as well as scope for creative activities such as origami, art, music, theatre, and nature walks.

Each Ikhvelo is led by an Ikhvelo in-charge who is generally a senior sahbhagi from within the village where the Ikhvelo is located. The Ikhvelo in-charge is engaged in several tasks inside and outside the Ikhvelo. For one, he/she organises various learning events and activities for adolescents in and around the village. He/she also helps tutor students who are preparing for the Classes VIII and X open school examination.

The review in Desuri and Bassi in 2013 and Bap and Bali in 2016 note the following:

> The Ikhvelo is clearly a resource in the village, and children benefit from its presence in their midst. The various activities organised through the Ikhvelo increase their awareness and skills. Children who had come for the meeting at the Ikhvelo mentioned enjoying the library and the games at the Ikhvelo. 'We can talk and ask freely over here—*Didi* teaches us many things', said some children. The Ikhvelo in-charge is also linked with the youth group and is able to provide guidance to the group. It was observed that children drop in at the Ikhvelo directly after school. The in-charge mentioned that they like to play or read books when they come. When asked why they did not go home directly, the in-charge at Sambhariya library in Desuri block said that if they went home they would invariably be asked to do some work at home. Here, they were free to play. (Sinha 2013: 14)

> The Ikhvelos are spacious and well equipped, and most of the equipment seems to be in working condition. Computers were functional and internet connectivity too was available. Children were seen involved in Google searches for information related to school subjects, both as part of the Institute of Technical Education (ITE) programme as well as from their own interest and motivated by the Ikhvelo in-charge. The science equipment seemed to be in use and in good condition. Evidence of successfully conducted Science Fairs was available in the form of photos and videos and also narrated by the children themselves. There was also evidence as well as

> narration of the use of Ikhvelos by the community for applications, forms, making printouts and copies, etc. (Srinivasan 2016: 7–8)

At present, there are 24 Ikhvelos running in DD blocks. In the year 2016–17, they have reached out to 2,296 adolescents, 1,994 community members, and 468 children in the age group 6–10 years.

Village Learning Centres and Jhola Pustakalya

Village Learning Centres are functional at the village level and provide a learning environment to the adolescents. Most of these centres are located in hamlets where there is an absence of a learning environment. The centres have been facilitating the adolescents to experience learning through different activities, building relationship with their peers, and getting access to books in the library.

Promoting Women's Group and Jagrat Mahila Sangh

Gender equity and women's empowerment have been overarching principles that have guided DD activities. Therefore, working with women has been intrinsic to the project and also seen as essential part of working with adolescents. In the early years, regular meetings were held in the project area that led to women emerging as leaders and taking up issues related to women and their development. For example, in Kishanganj, work began with the revival of older women's groups, which were formed under Lok Jumbish project, and a Jagrit Mahila Sanghatan was formed, whereas in Bap, given the socio cultural milieu, formation of women's collective presented several challenges as women led restrictive lives with limited mobility.

The role of women groups has also been crucial in the context of social change and development. Understanding this need, conscious and continuous efforts have been made to facilitate the formation, strengthening and empowering women groups at the village and block levels. Over time, some of the women's groups have come together for resolving village-level issues, such as problems with the water and electricity supply; they have also taken action against cases of violence against women.

The Jagrat Mahila Sangh (JMS) is a federation of women's groups in each block, with representatives from each mahila samooh. JMS meetings are held once every two months. The JMS functions like a platform where women bring problems that they encounter in their villages. Possible solutions to these problems are discussed, and the meetings provide an opportunity for information sharing. Solutions proposed at the meeting are followed up by action by the concerned mahila samooh.

In the case of social issues, the federation comes together for action as a collective, and makes representation to local officials for public action against violence against women, social entitlements, or illicit liquor. In such a case, the DD team also plays a supportive role.

> In Abu road, the Mahila Manch organized a campaign for liquor prohibition because it realized that one of the main factors that led to the increase in the number of fights and accidents occurring in the village was the intake of alcohol. The consumption of alcohol had increased because the number of liquor shops had multiplied in the village. Kishori and women groups of DD led the campaign for alcohol prohibition in 25 villages. Five more panchayats joined the campaign as a ripple effect this year. In the panchayats of Jambdi, Taleti, Bahadurpura, Uplakhejada, and Nichalagarh, government contracts have been completely prohibited through the PESA act. The campaign was a big success and culminated in the closure of 10 wine shops in the villages. (DD Annual Report 2016–17: 25)

In the 2010 Panchayat elections, the Jagrit Mahila Sanghatan also prepared their election manifesto and contested the elections. In all, 11 women were elected as Sarpanch and 50 were elected as ward panch.

Working with Youth Collectives

Collectivising youth around a range of issues has been taken up throughout the project period. A youth Yuva Shakti Sanghatan evolved in Kishanganj block to provide an institutional base to adolescents to demand their rights such as right to work, right to information, right to live with human dignity and equality, and to enable youth to take action in the case of exploitation and injustice. Yuva Shakti Sangh (YSS) later came up in all intervention blocks.

Youth organisations comprising adolescent girls and boys are promoted at the village level with the objective of taking up social and development issues. These often emerge after youth have participated in one of the residential trainings and wish to come together for social and development action. In its early stages, a youth group identifies problems that they can address within their local context.

The activities undertaken by the youth groups have included getting various benefits for the village, such as ensuring National Rural Employment Guarantee Act (NREGA) work, accessing entitlements like old age pension, installation of hand pumps, appointment of second teacher for the school, and taking up issues like child marriage and dowry. Representatives from the youth forums meet regularly at the YSS meetings held monthly. The objective of the YSS is to build a visible collective youth strength at the block level to take up social action.

A recent addition to programme activities has been in the sphere of livelihoods. Linkages have been made for vocational training. Around 500 adolescents have been linked to various vocational training institutions including the ICICI Academy for Skill training. This component follows organically from the other inputs provided to adolescents.

Partnerships with Government

DD has been working closely with panchayats and government school systems in the intervention blocks. A number of trainings and activities are organised with students and teachers. Teacher trainings have focussed on the importance of quality education, retention of children in the school, provision of different facilities in school, SMC formation and its strengthening process, school development plan, and providing information on Right to Education Act.

Students enrolled in schools are also actively involved in various DD activities at the Ikhevelo centres.

Emergence as a Resource Group and Centre

During the period 2014–17, DD is seeking to reach the last mile, extending resource services to other states, e.g. Jharkhand, eastern Uttar Pradesh, and southern Odhisa, in partnership with other NGOs that are also Trust partners. This also entails that the DD is geared to meet the new challenges in terms of pedagogy, course content, training, and communication.

Section II

Assessing Gains and Challenges

The DD initiative for adolescents has been innovative in character. The broader objective of DD has been facilitation of leadership among marginalised adolescents across geographical and cultural diversity. It has taken into account the needs of a large number of adolescents from disadvantaged communities who were out of schools and were not engaged in any academic activity. The project aimed to fill this gap by addressing educational concerns of this deprived group. The strategy adopted has been wide ranging. The target group was identified systematically and an effort made to bring together the relevant stakeholders, i.e. parents, community members, youth groups, women's groups, PRIs, teachers, and school management, who supported the process of social transformation.

Successive reviews undertaken at different strategies of project implementation show that the various strategies have been effective in raising awareness and confidence among adolescents who have participated or come in contact through residential camps, short-term training, or centres. It has also enabled a large number of adolescents to be linked to continuing education.

The broad gains that are discernible over the years are:

Creating New Opportunities for Learning

The DD camps have provided an opportunity for the Sahbhagis to reflect, analyse, and articulate their concerns and also led to awareness on a range of issues. The camps have provided an atmosphere of equity and freedom to girls and boys who have led restrictive lives. The various continuing education initiatives supported by the women's and youth groups have led to collective action for communitarian gains. The micro-planning processes have also helped in monitoring the gains.

It is clearly evident that the project enabled a change in attitudes regarding the need for education, especially of girls. The fact that a large number of girls have participated in the residential trainings with parental support and consent has been a significant step. The parents and community members observed the changes in the boys and girls who attended the camps and encouraged the adolescents to study further.

Many of the adolescents who have graduated from the residential camps have been motivated to pursue higher education.

1. Parsi from Bali Block joined the 4-month camp as an illiterate. She is now working with DD as a master trainer. She has completed her post-graduation.
2. Ravi had to drop out of school in Grade 3 after the death of his father. He belonged to a SC family. In 2007, he came in contact with the DD team of Bassi block and joined the 4-month residential camp. The project team members and his mother motivated him to continue his education after the camp. He continued his studies and completed Class VIII and then X from Open Middle School with the help of DD. At present, Ravi is enrolled in BA 3rd year in a full-time regular course.

3. Seema Garasiya from Pindwara block had never been to school before she joined the DD 4-month camp. She has completed her graduation and is now aspiring to be an IAS officer.

   (Adapted from Report of the Forum, DD 2016)

Promoting Community Ownership and Involvement

The DD experience indicates that that a well-designed intervention that delivers quality education will be readily accepted by the community. Without the ownership and involvement of communities, adolescent initiatives are at best half-way houses. The intensive community engagement at various levels has helped create a supportive environment for promoting adolescent education. Communities have trusted DD processes to send their children to residential camps.

Reinforcing Learning through Integrated Education

In DD, education has meant taking into account a range of things. The environment provided in the residential camps has given a number of disadvantaged adolescents an opportunity to live and learn together. Each learner is supported by a group of dedicated trainers. The focus has been on providing holistic education wherein the adolescents developed an understanding of gender equality, rights, reproductive health, and life skills and civic and political education through educational programmes organised for them. It has given adolescents an opportunity to articulate their concerns and find solutions for them. It also helped them to bring about changes in their attitudes and values on issues of caste, class, and religion. It has also developed articulation, self-confidence, and the ability to engage in meaningful relationships with a variety of persons.

The current focus is also on integrating technology to improve the quality of DD programmes.

Sensitising the Local Institutions and Government Delivery System

The activities carried out in the project have given an opportunity to work closely with various government departments and

Panchayati Raj System. The various training programmes with teachers and students in schools have enabled taking forward new ideas about teaching and learning into the government system. This close association also led to the teachers providing support during camps or whenever necessary.

The project experience clearly brings out that any transformatory process should put in place linkages at multiple levels. One of the positive outcomes of the project has been that integrated education was sought to be achieved through a range of activities—camps, continuing learning centres, linkages with schools, formation of youth groups, and so on.

Challenges

The overall experience of DD suggests that providing holistic education integrated to lives of adolescents in a context of multiple disadvantages and deprivation can be extremely challenging. The demands raised at the field level are extensive.

In the Forum organised by DD in 2016, some of the issues that were raised included:

1. Transition of adolescents, especially girls, to secondary school;
2. Improving linkages and strengthening convergence with government schemes and programmes;
3. Strengthening community-based structures for effective implementation of government programmes and schemes at the grass root level;
4. Operations research to inform programming; and
5. Support for shared forums for learning.

References

Doosra Dashak (2016), *Report on Forum on Equity in Education for Adolescents: The case of Doosra Dashak (A vision for Future)*, Jaipur: Doosra Dashak.

—— (2017a), *Annual Report (2016-2017)*, Jaipur: Doosra Dashak, FED.

—— (2017b), *Doosra Dashak: Parichay evam Prakriyaien*, Jaipur: FED.

Rajagopal, S. and V. Chakravarthy (2016), *State Strategy and Action Plan on Child Marriage: Rajasthan*, draft submitted to UNFPA, Jaipur: Rajasthan State Office.

Saldhana, D. (2007), *Education of Adolescents for Development in India: The Case of Doosra Dashak*, Jaipur: Rawat Publications.

Sinha, T. (2013), *Educating Adolescents and Youth for Community Development: A Doosra Dashak Programme (April 2010 to March 2013)*, Jaipur: Doosra Dashak.

Srinivasan, M. (2016), *One-Year Review of FED's Doosra Dashak Field Programme in Bap and Bali and Central Training Unit in Pisangan*, Jaipur: Doosra Dashak.

5

An Approach to Existential and Integrated Education for Youth

Case Study of SIDH

Pawan Gupta

At *Society of Integrated development of Himalayas* (SIDH), 'values' are never taught as a separate subject. They are therefore integrated, if I may say so. We learnt this from Mahatma Gandhi and also from the approach he took in *Nai Taleem* or *Buniyadi Shiksha.*

Just like categories, subjects are inventions of human beings. We categorise learning according to our convenience at a particular point in time and give them different names as different subjects. These subjects or categories and their scope and boundaries keep changing with time. For instance, the geography today is very different from the geography a few decades ago.

But learning and the desire to know and understand is an intrinsic human trait, not man-made. Human beings are, by nature, curious and want to know. Hence, to know and to understand, to stretch the boundaries of what is known, is intrinsic to nature of human beings.

Therefore, at SIDH, we have taken this approach of keeping the object centre stage and weave different subjects as and when required, in the process of learning. Subjects like textbooks are only a 'means' to acquire knowledge and actually these days mostly information. The objective is to acquire knowledge. Therefore, an integrated approach to teaching and learning is more natural and in alignment with the existential order. As we understand, *Nai Taleem* takes a similar approach, and we derived support and confidence from that.

We were also not comfortable with the manner in which values are generally 'taught' in our schools. Values, unlike other subjects, are neither 'means' nor categories. Values are intrinsic to human beings. Every human being needs food but with respect. This intrinsic need of human beings, universal as it is has not been given adequate attention in our education system. At the physiological and biological levels, attention has been given, but at the non-material level, where we all are the same, the common among us, these aspects have been ignored, barring exceptions like the subject of psychology, perhaps. But this too largely deals with preparing the individual to 'adjust', make sort of peace with the way things are, in this increasingly aggressive, competitive, and exploitative world order.

The basic human nature, emotional needs, and desire for respect, trust, glory, love, gratitude, etc. are common to all humanity irrespective of caste, gender, race, culture, and economic differences. This aspect is not being dealt adequately in our education system. These values, if we would like to call them by that name, are not 'duties' but intrinsic 'needs' of human beings. The need to give and get respect, trust, and love is intrinsic. Whenever these feelings are aroused in us, we feel good and happy. We humans are designed like that. And anything that is intrinsic and therefore existential can be seen, felt, and understood by anyone, if it were appropriately pointed out. So this was our approach to show, to reveal the existential, the real, what is rather than teach values. In our system, the word 'should' was shunned.

In India, this technique or method was known as *dhyanakarshan vidhi* (ध्यानाकर्षण विधि). The teacher attempted to draw the attention of the children to see the truth, as it is/was like a finger pointing to the moon. The student would ultimately have to make a personal attempt to see where the teacher's finger was pointing, the object. Teachers can only do so much, indicate through different techniques or methods, no more. This becomes even more relevant when dealing in the non-material or the intangible domain. But once the students see the object being pointed out, then nothing can shake their confidence. That is the power of truth, once revealed.

Values are non-material. For instance, respect or trust or love, how do you make the student understand them? The act or demonstration of respect in the form of namaskar, shaking of hands, touching of feet, etc. are not respect but at best manifestation of respect. But what is respect? The question remains. Also, the action (for respect or trust or love) can be false. To understand the value, one has to look within, understand and feel the qualitative aspect, the 'being' aspect and not the 'doing' aspect (the act). To understand the intangible, the non-material, it is essential to look within and be introspective. It is worth pointing out that our present mainstream education is entirely outward looking. This practice tends to confuse information with knowledge. Information has to be sought outside, whereas knowledge has to be gained and internalised.

At SIDH, we created a list of sets of distinctions to help students examine their hidden assumptions. These were discussed and pointed out whenever the opportunity arose, while teaching. A few examples:

Meaning and Word; Listening (to the meaning) and Hearing (the Word); Dialogue and Debate; Responsibility and Right; Objective and Means; What, Why, and How; Swatantrta (freedom with self-discipline through understanding) and Freedom; Truth (eternal) and Fact (transitory); Knowledge and Information; Knowledge and Skill; Education and Literacy; Agreement/disagreement on Meaning (of the other) or the Words (of the other); *Desh* (country and the local, no fixed boundaries) and *Rashtra* (Nation State); Patriotism (*desh bhakti*) and Nationalism (*Rashtra bhakti*); Value and Price; and Getting inspired and getting influenced/impressed.

The list was carefully prepared. Both the words in the list were related but had very distinct meanings. Mostly there was confusion between the two. One was the manifest or doing aspect, and the other was the real/intrinsic/being/more grounded aspect. One could be easily seen/learnt, but the other had to be felt and understood (within).

These are a few examples to give an idea of our technique of *dhyanakarshan.* It was successful opening of the minds and getting the students to look within to find answers. This encouraged them to self-reflect. This resulted in (real) learning, giving the students self-confidence.

Our approach was not structured or organic in nature. We used speeches and writings from *The Collected Works of Mahatma Gandhi*. The emphasis was not so much on his words as on understanding the context in which he said or wrote and then to the understanding of the foundational logic behind his thoughts. The students could appreciate where he was coming from and feel his deep respect for the ordinary Indian villager, the value system of our ordinary people, Mahatma's courage, and the source of his confidence and understanding. We used 'Hind Swaraj' extensively to deconstruct modernity. This encouraged students to look behind the obvious and see the reality. In this, we were helped by some of the people who gave us tremendous support, such as Ven. Samdong Rinpoche, Late Shri Kishan Patnayak, Late Sri Dharampal, Late Sri A. Nagraj, Dhiru Bhai, Surabhi Sheth, and many others.

We never relied on popular names or so-called 'experts' and professionals. Rather we tried to gauge the sincerity and authenticity in the person to share whatever they felt like and we hardly ever went wrong. They could be from any field as long as they had something to share. The idea was never to 'teach' but help them 'see' for themselves. It was an unconventional approach, full of risks but it worked. The authenticity and sincerity of these people had a huge impact on the students. The discussions were not just passing of information but turned into experiential learning. It was transformative.

Working with hands, dignity of labour, and production activity were given the importance they deserved. We tried to weave in subjects like maths, local knowledge, science, environmental science, agriculture, health, hygiene, economics, and even world politics while teaching how to make or produce things. For instance, while making biscuits or bread in our bakery, we could discuss economics and market forces, the related health issues, and purity/impurity in food items. We never took a linear approach.

By pointing out the wisdom hidden in their local language, in their idioms, phrases, and stories, they started to appreciate their own, which normally gets discarded almost instinctively as backward, without proper examination, under the influence of modernity.

We used newspapers and magazines extensively. The same news item or comment (in editorials) on the same topic carried in different magazines and newspapers never matched with one another. They were made to read these varied reports and then discuss which one was correct or incorrect. Slowly a confidence in their capacity to grasp things evolved.

The idea behind most of our effort was to give the students real self-confidence through understanding and knowledge and liberating them from false notions, which give them inferiority complex and a sense that they are not good enough, that they are backward, that they are victims. Ours has been an ongoing teaching/learning approach where we constantly learnt from our efforts and observations and were always open to try out new methods.

In the beginning, the students were a bit lost as they were not used to this out-of-the-box process of learning. It required a lot of encouragement. But we kept on exposing the hidden assumptions that they were carrying about 'development', about 'backwardness', about our languages vis-à-vis English, about the wisdom and knowledge existing in our very own culture especially about health, food, knowledge in agricultural practices, etc. Slowly they started feeling and experiencing a sense of ease with themselves, with their background, which hitherto they felt embarrassed or shy about. This prepared them for receiving learning and knowledge. Normally, the lack of confidence, feeling embarrassed or inferior, diffidence, and hidden false assumptions are great impediments to receiving knowledge. These negatives block the receiving. Once these obstacles are removed, a natural unfolding happens, provided there is a conducive environment, which indicates or points towards what already lies within.

6

Health Concerns of Adolescents in India

Narendra Gupta

Adolescence is a phase between childhood and adulthood. It lays the foundation of the economic and social future of individuals as also the contribution they will make to the society. The rapid changes occurring in an individual's biology and psychology are a significant factor for considering the health perspective as critical. This paper discusses health-related issues of this group with greater attention to rural adolescents.

Defining Adolescents and Their Health

Adolescents ought to be considered a very important segment of the society as they largely determines the demographic and economic profile of the country. Broadly, persons aged between 10 and 19 years are termed as adolescents, but some of the various agencies and departments concerned with their development employ different age ranges. The two generally recognised subgroups for delivery of services are 10–14 years and 15–19 years as the two groups are marked by distinct service requirements. Adolescents as a group constitute approximately

21 per cent of the total Indian population, but this proportion varies from state to state. It is obviously correlated to the rate of population growth—the higher the growth rate, the greater is the proportion of adolescents in the population.

Table 1

States with the Highest and Lowest Proportions of Adolescents

Five Highest	*Adolescent Proportion (%)*	*Five Lowest*	*Adolescent Proportion (%)*
Uttar Pradesh	24.5	Andhra Pradesh	19.3
Rajasthan	22.9	Maharashtra	19.0
Uttarakhand	22.5	Karnataka	18.9
Bihar	22.5	Tamil Nadu	17.2
Jharkhand	22.2	Kerala	16.3

Source: Census of India, 2011

Adolescence follows childhood, when a person begins to have a mind of her/his own. Rapid changes in the body, behaviour, and cognitive faculties occur during this period. Gender, social category, economic status, and geography are among the prime factors that affect a person's physical, behavioural, and cognitive development. Changes in adolescents are largely influenced by their childhood, informed by the socio-economic realities of their families. A child of an economically poor family from a socially excluded community residing in a remote location would be quite different in physique, mental orientation, skills, and social abilities when it enters adolescence as compared with a child of a better-off family with greater acceptance into the society. Adolescents also experience gender differentiation with the onset of puberty and sexual awakening.

Adolescents are generally healthy unless they suffer from an ailment contracted in childhood. Yet, many deaths occur during this period, a majority of which are preventable. The leading causes of adolescent deaths in India are road accidents, self-harm, diarrheal diseases, human immunodeficiency virus infection and acquired immune deficiency syndrome, lower respiratory tract infections, and meningitis. Many deaths and morbidities preceding them could be attributed to poverty, lack of education, social discrimination, early marriage, and teenage pregnancies.

Adolescent health concerns arise broadly from reproductive and sexual issues, mental issues, and nutritional issues.

Reproductive and Sexual Health

Adolescents experience physical changes—growth of height, weight, reproductive organs, and pubic hair; and onset of menstruation, development of mammary glands, changes in pelvic structure (all among girls); and facial hair and crackling of voice among boys. The onset of menstruation (called menarche) indicates that the girl is able to conceive. Most girls are not adequately prepared for it. They could experience hormone-induced mood swings, which could be sometimes negative.

Topics of sexuality and reproduction both for girls and boys are mostly considered taboo and not talked about. This pushes adolescents to explore and experiment with them on their own without proper guidance. Another important issue is unsafe sex leading to teenage pregnancies within or outside marriage as knowledge of and access to contraception devices is limited. Teenage pregnancies within marriage could lead to an increase in the number and more frequency of pregnancies, which pose big risks to the health of the young mother-to-be.

Teenage pregnancies outside marriage may lead to unsafe abortion. According to the National Family Health Survey (NFHS) 4 conducted in 2015–16, 26.8 per cent of Indian women in the age group of 20–24 years were married before they were 18. This statistic is even higher in rural areas (31.5 per cent). Some 20.3 per cent of the men (24.4 per cent in rural areas) in the age range of 25–29 years were married before the legal age of marriage for men (21 years). The proportion of teenage pregnancies had halved, from 16.0 per cent in NFHS 3 to 7.9 per cent in NFHS 4, but the absolute number was still high, around 11.8 million.

Table 2

Reproductive and Sexual Health Status of Indian Adolescents

Factors	*Male (%)*	*Female (%)*
Sexual initiation under the age of 15 years*	2.7	8.0
Contraceptive awareness (15–19 years)*	96.0	94.0
Ever used contraceptives*	29.4	40.4
Condom used during first time*	19.0	3.0
Delivered baby before age 18 (2008–12)#	–	21.7
Comprehensive knowledge of HIV*	34.5	18.6
STI** or symptoms of STI in sexually active adolescents*	10.8	10.5
Prevalence of HIV among adolescents*	0.0	0.1

Sources: *NFHS 3, **Sexually Transmitted Infections and #UNICEF

Nutrition

Adolescents require wholesome and balanced food rich in calories, proteins, and micro-nutrients because of their rapid physical growth. But they suffer from anaemia and malnutrition just as much as the bulk of Indian population does. NFHS 3 estimated nearly 56 per cent of the girls and 30 per cent of the boys to be anaemic. The situation has improved since then, but a quarter of all girls and boys still suffer from moderate to severe anaemia. A large number are undernourished as they lack food. They fall sick repeatedly and suffer from chronic diseases such as tuberculosis. Nearly half the adolescent girls and three-fifths of the boys are underweight. At the same time, over consumption and obesity, insignificant until a decade ago, are also rising. Increasing consumption of junk food rich in trans-fats along with adulteration and contamination of food is the most likely reason for this. NFHS 4 records that 20 per cent of the women and 19 per cent of the men in the age range of 15–49 years have body mass index above 25.

Mental Health

Issues relating to mental health are the most neglected among adolescents. Morbidity and mortality caused by depression have increased substantially in recent years. Several reasons including the proliferation of electronic and social media are responsible for this. The adolescent suicidal behaviour can be attributed to factors such as sexual abuse, premarital sex, hesitant independent decision-making, absenteeism, and mental disorders. The pressure to perform and conform to peer norms is the highest in adolescents amongst all age groups. Most adolescents from socio-economically marginalised sections face pressing problems of earning and adding to the family income. They sometimes migrate from their homes in search of jobs. Some who undertake risky jobs could be prone to substance abuse.

Substance Abuse

Both the percentage and absolute numbers of adolescent users of tobacco products, alcohol, and cannabis and other psychotropic drugs are rising. According to NFHS 3, 11 per cent of adolescent boys and 1 per cent of adolescent girls had consumed alcohol; about 3 per cent consumed it daily. The average age at the initial use of tobacco was 12.3 years and that of alcohol is 13.6 years. Some 11 per cent of cannabis users started at 15. Alarming as these figures are, the greater tragedy is that most users have little knowledge of the consequences of their habits.

Accidental and Intentional Violence

Various surveys conducted in different parts of India aver that nearly three-fourths of the adolescents, especially boys, engage in risky behaviour, such as not following traffic rules, leading to grievous injuries and even death. Use of helmets while riding two wheelers and seat belts in four wheelers is not followed, increasing the possibilities of fatal injuries including to the head even in not-so-serious accidents. Sexual abuse is also a big concern, not just for girls but also for boys. This phenomenon is mostly not reported and victims suffer in silence, fearing social stigma. This affects the growth of the person physically, mentally, and socially.

Adolescent Health Programmes and Challenges

For long, adolescence was not considered a distinct category from the health perspective. Only contraception and services for pregnancy and maternal health were considered as worthy of attention. The Reproductive and Child Health programme of 1997 saw the start of adolescent clinics in secondary public health institutions as part of the Adolescent Reproductive and Sexual Health (ARSH) programme. But services could not be delivered to adolescents in the manner envisaged for want of adequate financial and human resources. There was no direct access, or private space, or fixed schedule for ARSH services. Service providers did not receive proper training for understanding the perspective, skills, and sensitivity needed for component activities.

Adolescents have no notion of counselling on their health-related matters. Generally, they are unwilling to discuss their physical and sexual health or to be examined by healthcare providers of the opposite sex. This concern of privacy acts as an impediment for services reaching them. These lacunae in the implementation of adolescent health activities are corroborated by the fact that there has not been any significant improvement in the physical, mental, and social health. In fact, there are signs of rises in instances of gender-based violence, teenage pregnancies, and substance abuse.

ARSH implemented through adolescent-friendly health services in secondary institutions has been turned into Rashtriya Kishore Swasthya Karyakram since 2014. But different activities are still carried out by different ministries and departments unlike what the design envisaged. The programme is lagging behind in meeting its objectives due also to inadequate financial allocations.

Issues Involved

The current allocation of a mere 1 per cent of the GDP for health services in general is grossly insufficient. Comprehensive adolescent health services cannot be provided without sizeable augmentation of resources.

Table 3

Programmes/Schemes of Ministry of Health and Family Welfare

Name	*Services Offered*
Rashtriya Kishor Swasthya Karyakram	Improve physical health
	Improve sexual and reproductive health
	Prevent injuries and violence
	Prevent substance abuse
	Enhance mental health
Rashtriya Bal Swasthya Karyakram for children up to 18 years	Health screening
	Promotion of healthy lifestyle
	Identification of development delays

Table 4

Programmes/Schemes of Ministry of Women and Child Development

Name	*Services Offered*
Kishori Shakti Yojna for adolescent girls	Improve nutritional, health, and overall development
	Promote awareness of health, hygiene, nutrition, and family care
	Linked with opportunities for learning life skills and going back to school
	Help to gain better understanding of social environment
	Support initiatives to become productive members of the society
Balika Samridhi Yojna	To enhance marriage age and re-enrolment in schools
Rajiv Gandhi Scheme for Empowerment of Adolescent Girls Sabla	Implemented in 200 districts with the objective to improve health and hygiene and life skills through *anganwadis*

Adolescents are at the intersection of the National Policy for Children, which covers all those below 18 as children, and the National Policy for Youth, which treats persons between 15 and 29 as youth. As a result, there is a danger of their missing out from either category. India needs a context- and location-specific multi-dimensional approach to address health concerns of adolescents with skilled and motivated service providers. To facilitate their needs, all public health institutions should include adolescent-friendly service centres.

Table 5

Programmes/Schemes of Other Ministries

Name	*Services Offered*
Narcotics Drugs and Psychotropic Substances Act, 1985	Awareness and prevention
The Cigarettes and Other Tobacco Products (Prohibition of Advertisement and Regulation of Trade and Commerce, Production, Supply and Distribution) Act, 2003	Awareness and prevention

Complete adolescent health screening at regular intervals and their involvement in health matters relating to them should be ensured. A comprehensive data set exclusively for adolescents needs to be created urgently for monitoring and formulation of specific adolescent health programmes.

7

Policies and Programmes on Adolescent Health in India

Structure of Opportunities for Adolescents

S. Ramanathan and Vasudha Chakravarthy

Health is among the important needs of adolescents. The government has recognised this over the past two decades or so and has tried to address it. This paper documents key government policies and interventions and examines the issues that remain.

The Context of Adolescent Health in India

Not just the notion of adolescence but the very phase itself is intriguing for the adolescents, parents, service providers, and others. It is a period of vulnerability in India as culturally one is either a child or an adult. The passage from childhood to adulthood is usually defined by the marital status. Hence, a married girl at 15 years of age ceases to be an adolescent. There is a significant degree of non-acceptance of the phase of adolescence in the Indian society. And, this has a bearing on access to services including education, mobility, and behaviour. Due to this non-acceptance or the recognition of the adolescent phase, sexuality outside marriage is often not accepted or recognised.

This has an impact on the provision of information and services. Adult gatekeepers often tend to resort to denial of information as a protective strategy.

However, because of increasing education levels and higher age at marriage, the gap between age at menarche and age at parenthood is increasing significantly. Hence, the adolescents as a group are becoming an increasing reality in India.

While there is no universally accepted definition of adolescence, the United Nations has defined an adolescents to be in the age group of 10–19 years. Based on this definition, adolescents constitute about 20 per cent of the population. The proportion of adolescents in the Indian population has remained at 21 per cent since 1971.[1]

The adolescents are a diverse population segment. One, they are in different stages of development—early, mid, or late adolescence. Two, there are both married and unmarried adolescents. Three, they live in different contexts and different living conditions: urban, peri-urban, and rural, and those who live in the street or workers. Adolescents are thus marked by diverse needs, issues, and concerns.

Young people are usually regarded as healthy. Therefore, excessive concern for their health may seem misplaced. However, the period of adolescence coincides with significant changes in their physique and determinants of health, which impact later in life. For instance, according to the World Health Organization (WHO), more than 33 per cent of the disease burden and about 60 per cent of the premature deaths among adults can be associated with the behaviour or conditions that began or occurred during adolescence.[2] The disability-adjusted life years lost due to vulnerabilities such as sexual abuse and violence, injuries (both self-inflicted and intimate partner violence), gender-linked violence, early pregnancy, and maternal mortality are significant. The *Lancet* also provided evidence that a preventive approach during adolescence reduces mental health problems and lowers substance misuse, as does consistent condom use lead to fewer sexually transmitted infections (STIs).

Another reason to focus on the health and education of adolescents is that they represent a significant demographic dividend for the country.

The key health vulnerabilities of adolescents include:

1. Sexual and reproductive health;
2. Malnutrition and anaemia;
3. Mental health;
4. Substance misuse and abuse;
5. Injuries; and
6. Violence, including intimate partner violence.

In view of their transition to adulthood and impending parenthood, their sexual and reproductive health needs have received greater attention. Many marry at an age lower than the legal minimum and are initiated early into sexual relations within marriage with consequences such as early childbearing; no or less space between births, and deaths due to maternal disorders. Deaths due to abortion are an added hazard. Women in the age group of 15–24 years account for over 46 per cent of all maternal deaths in the country. The contraceptive needs of young married couples are far from being met. And, given the increasing gap between age at menarche and parenthood, pre-marital sex is prevalent. Apart from early initiation to sex among some adolescents, there is also an issue of multiple partners. Studies indicate that over the years, there is a substantial increase in number of adolescents reporting pre-marital sexual experiences. And, among those who are sexually active prior to marriage, the contraceptive use, specifically its consistent use, is low.

Even as the adolescents' sexual and reproductive health needs are significant, they have other needs too. A large proportion of India's adolescents are anaemic: 56 per cent of girls and 30 per cent of boys.[3] Obesity and overweight are growing concerns, especially in urban areas. Mental health is also an issue: WHO reports that about 25 per cent of the adolescents in the age group of 13–15 years (constituting about

6 per cent of the population) were depressed; 11 per cent were distracted (unable to focus on studies or homework); 8 per cent suffered from anxiety; 8 per cent were lonely; and 10 per cent had no close friends. The estimated suicide rate per 1,00,000 was 35.5 among those aged between 15 and 29 years. Parental involvement reduced mental health issues but bullying by peers or friends in schools aggravated it (WHO 2014).

Substance misuse, injuries, and violence are some other problems. Globally, about 52 per cent of deaths among male adolescents and about 30 per cent among female adolescents are due to injuries. Growing instances of violence, especially sexual violence, against young women are reported in the media.

While their health needs are many and varied, according to many studies, adolescents possess only limited awareness and information on these issues. Most rely on their peers and, to a lesser extent, the media for information. A very small proportion appears to have been exposed to education on sexuality.

Overview of Policies and Programmes on Adolescent Health

Contrary to the non-acceptance of this phase of adolescence in the society, there has been a better recognition of adolescents and their needs in the government policies and programmes. The adolescents' need to make informed choice and take responsible decisions is recognised by the government. This is also reflected in government commitments to various agencies such as the International Conference on Population and Development of the United Nations Population Fund (UNFPA).

The Working Group on Adolescents for the Tenth Five-Year Plan (2002–07) mentioned that:

> There is growing evidence of tremendous lack of awareness of their bodies and sexual behaviour, both among boys and girls, and there is considerable interest among them in filling this gap in knowledge. What is, therefore, urgently required for both adolescent girls and adolescent boys are programmes which help deal with their own well-being, their health, their

> bodies, and their sexual lives ... and in the light of growing evidence of ignorance in sexual matters on the one hand and considerable sexual activity among young unmarried people on the other. (Planning Commission 2001)

It also said that adolescents have a right to information about their bodies, diseases and their prevention, reproduction, transmission of diseases and how they can protect themselves, and a right to health care services, including reproductive health counselling and services (Planning Commission 2001: 35).

The impact of education and livelihood on health of adolescents was also recognised. The *National Population Policy, 2000, National AIDS Prevention and Control Policy, 2002*, and *National Youth Policy 2003* recognised the need to address young persons as a special and vulnerable group. The *National Policy on Education, 1986* (modified in 1992) and *National Skill Development Policy, 2009* have reiterated the need to equip young people with adequate schooling and skills to compete in a globalising world.

The key policy commitments for adolescents, with a focus on their health are:

The *National Population Policy, 2000* recognised for the first time that adolescents constitute an underserved group, with special health needs and advocated programmatic attention to address this subgroup. It outlined the need to ensure access to affordable services and information and counselling on reproductive health (Jejeebhoy and Santhya 2011). The need to ensure minimum age at marriage; prevent and control communicable diseases, especially acquired immune deficiency syndrome (AIDS) and STIs; and strengthen primary health care for provision of services and counselling were also emphasised (Mondal 2017).

The *National AIDS Prevention and Control Policy, 2002* highlighted the importance of better understanding of the human immunodeficiency virus (HIV) infection and safer sex among the young (National AIDS Control Organisation [NACO], 2002). The policy suggested awareness building, condom promotion, and creation of an enabling environment for prevention of HIV/AIDS. It advocated the provision of HIV/AIDS education in schools and colleges through curricular and co-curricular activities, as well as through youth organisations.

The *National Youth Policy, 2003* provided a comprehensive overview of the issues and concerns of youth and recognised adolescents as a special group. The policy centred on youth empowerment in different spheres of national life (*The National Youth Policy (2003)* 2015) and advocated youth participation—'working with youth and not merely for youth'. It stressed an inter-sectoral approach and the need for coordination among various departments and programmes, community block organisations, and youth bodies. The establishment of youth development centres to act as information centres for youth was also recommended. It advocated free counselling services and establishment of adolescent clinics and youth health associations.

The *National Youth Policy, 2014* reiterated the commitments of the 2003 policy and envisaged holistic development by addressing health, education, and livelihood needs of young persons. Enabling youth participation and civic engagement were emphasised. A healthy lifestyle, free of substance abuse and addiction, and prevention of harmful sexual practices were identified as the health focus areas. Comprehensive campaigns on issues such as HIV/AIDS, substance abuse, sanitation and hygiene, and nutrition and establishment of youth-friendly information centres were advocated.

The *National Health Policy, 2000* stressed in raising awareness of health-promoting behaviours among school and college students. The *National Health Policy, 2017* emphasised health challenges of adolescents and long-term benefits of investing in their health care. While recommending the strengthening of health systems for implementing the reproductive, maternal, newborn, child, and adolescent health activities, it also advocated expansion of healthcare for adolescents beyond sex and reproductive health to address other concerns such as inadequate calorie intake, nutrition status, and psychological problems linked to misuse of technology.[4]

Several other policies also recognise the needs of adolescents. The *National Nutrition Policy, 1983* focusses on the importance of nutrition for adolescent girls. The *National Policy for Empowerment of Women, 2001* covers aspects of nutrition, education, violence against the girl child, sexual abuse, and violation of rights of the girl child. The *National Policy on Education, 1986* (modified in 1992) emphasises the need for employment-related education and programmes to motivate and inform young people about family planning and responsible parenthood (Ministry of Human Resource Development, 1998).

A commitment to address needs of adolescents and young persons is also articulated in various 5-year plans. We have mentioned the Working Group on Adolescents for the Tenth Five-Year Plan (2002–07). The Eleventh Five-Year Plan (2007 12), too, recognised the importance of investing in adolescents. It noted that health needs of adolescents have been largely neglected. It recommended provision of youth- and adolescent-friendly services for creating awareness and providing information. The Twelfth Five-Year Plan (2012–17), while moving towards universal health coverage, stressed nutrition, preventive and protective health education, and improved service delivery for adolescents.[5]

Several programmes based on such policies address health needs of adolescent girls and boys. They can be broadly grouped into three categories: school-based, community-based, and clinic-based. Some of the key programmes are outlined below.

School-Based Programmes

Adolescence Education Programme (AEP) of the Ministry of Human Resource Development and NACO (2005) was implemented in 11,200 schools. Approximately 2,88,000 teachers were trained (Jejeebhoy and Santhya 2011).

The programme' objectives are to ensure first that all schools provide accurate, age-appropriate, life skills-based adolescence education in a sustained manner to young people (10–18 years) in schools. Further, it aimed to equip all children with accurate information, knowledge, and life skills to protect themselves from HIV and manage adolescent reproductive sexual health (ARSH) concerns. All out-of-school adolescents are to be provided basic information and services on ARSH, HIV prevention, and prevention of substance abuse. AEP also sought effective integration of adolescence education components in school curriculum as well as teacher education. It was to ensure that linkages to youth-friendly services are established and resources for additional information are easily accessible (*Adolescence Education Programme, Facilitators' Guide* 2017).

Unfortunately, serious reservations have been expressed about the sexual education component of the programme since 2006, and several states have banned it (Jejeebhoy and Santhya 2011). A revised curriculum was developed and implemented through State Councils of Educational Research and Training/State Boards in 2009–10. With support from UNFPA, it is also being implemented by several national agencies, such as the Central Board for Secondary Education, Navodaya Vidyalaya Samiti, Kendriya Vidyalaya Sangathan, National Institute of Open Schooling, and National Council of Educational Research and Training (NCERT). Several aspects of adolescent concerns have also been integrated into mainstream subjects by NCERT. AEP is also being implemented by several central schools across the country.

School Health Programme (SHP), 2008, promoted by National Rural Health Mission, comprises interventions to improve in-school adolescents' awareness of health, hygiene, and nutrition matters through curricular formats and of growing up issues and sexual and reproductive health matters through co-curricular approaches. The objectives of the programme are the promotion of positive health; the prevention of diseases; early diagnosis, treatment, and follow up of defects; and awakening health consciousness in children (*School Health Programme* 2008). The programme is being successfully implemented in Tamil Nadu, Kerala, Gujarat, and West Bengal (*Guidelines on School Health Programme* 2009).

SHP entails a biannual health screening and early management of disease, disability, common deficiencies and linkages with secondary and tertiary health facilities, as required. The effort is also to promote physical activity and counselling in the school, coupled with education. Fixed day immunisation is provided, along with weekly iron and folic acid supplementation and biannual deworming.

Community-Based Programmes

Kishori Shakti Yojna (KSY) was introduced by the Ministry of Women and Child Development in the year 2000. It aims to empower adolescent girls (aged 11–18 years), concentrating on out-of-school girls. It is a redesigned version of the adolescent girl's scheme, which sought to improve the health and nutrition status of adolescent girls and provide them vocational and life skills for economic empowerment.

SABLA, a part of the Rajiv Gandhi Scheme for Empowerment of Adolescent Girls, replaced KSY in 200 select districts in 2011. Continuing its focus on out-of-school adolescent girls, the programme is implemented through *anganwadi* centres for delivery of services. The objectives of SABLA are enabling self-development and empowerment of adolescent girls; improving their nutrition and health status; promoting awareness about health, hygiene, nutrition, ARSH, and family and child care; upgrading their home-based skills and life skills; tying up with National Skill Development Programme for vocational skills; mainstreaming out-of-school adolescent girls into formal/non-formal education; and finally, providing information/guidance about existing public services, such as primary health centres (PHC), community health centres (CHC), post offices, banks, and police stations (*SABLA* 2017). The *anganwadi* workers are expected to survey and register all adolescent girls within their jurisdictions and gather them for regular meetings and service provision at the centres.

National Programme for Youth and Adolescent Development, implemented by the Ministry of Youth Affairs and Sports, is another notable scheme that aims to provide enabling opportunities for holistic development of young persons. One of the key objectives of the scheme is to empower adolescents through life-skills education, counselling and career guidance, using residential camps to provide a second chance to acquire basic education.

Other efforts include the *Village Talk AIDS* programme, a part of the National AIDS Control Programme (NACP) II. The Nehru Yuva Kendra Sangathan has also conducted awareness campaigns on sexual and reproductive health and HIV/AIDS. NACP III established rural resource centres for youth-oriented counselling. The Ministry of Youth Affairs and Sports formed 3,824 teen clubs in 64 districts, with support from UNFPA. They act as a vehicle for young people to acquire life skills-focussed experiential learning on reproductive and sexual health issues, along with information on education and skill building for employability.

Clinic-Based Programmes

Adolescent Sexual and Reproductive Health Strategy and Programme was first launched in 2005 as a part of the reproductive and child health activities of the National Health Mission. It sought to reorganise the existing public health system to meet the health needs of adolescents through provision of health services in identified Adolescent Friendly Health Centres across the country. Preventive, protective, curative, and outreach services were made available to all adolescents.

Two levels of care for young people was envisaged: routine subcentre clinics run by female health workers and weekly 2-hour clinics organised at the PHC/CHC/district level run by the health worker and medical officer. At the subcentre level, the health worker was to provide non-terminal contraceptive methods, routine antenatal care services, abortion-related referrals, reproductive and sexually transmitted infections (RTI-STI)/HIV-related education, nutritional counselling, information on menstrual hygiene, and immunisation of pregnant adolescents. The clinics will offer such services as contraceptive supplies, management of menstrual disorders, RTI/STI preventive education and management, pregnancy termination and related counselling, nutritional counselling, and counselling for sexual problems (Jejeebhoy and Santhya 2011). The strategy also recommended a monthly awareness-raising activity for youth to be undertaken by auxiliary nurse midwives, *anganwadi* women workers, accredited social health activists, youth group coordinators, and male health workers.

Rashtriya Kishor Swasthya Karyakram (RKSK), launched in 2014, sought to improve and expand the ARSH programme. It caters to all adolescents, in and out of school, married and unmarried, rural and urban. It has six strategic priorities: nutrition, Sexual and Reproductive Health (SRH), non-communicable diseases, substance misuse, injuries and violence (including gender-related violence), and mental health (Johnson 2014).

The programme also comprises community-based interventions through peer educators. It envisages to be holistic and participative, providing adolescents leadership, equity, and inclusion opportunities and strategic partnerships with other sectors and stakeholders.

Policies, Programmes, and Empowering Opportunities for Adolescent Health

We define empowerment as an ability to make effective choices, i.e. the ability to translate choices into desired actions and outcomes. This is influenced by two factors, the agency and opportunity structure.

The agency is the person or organisation making choices. The opportunity structure is the context in which persons are situated, which could be formal or informal. Agency indicates the ability of a person to make choices; in other words, the person can determine the various options and make a choice. Opportunity structure is the context in which persons are situated and this could be both formal and informal contexts. Together, they lead to different degrees of empowerment. In the context of adolescent health, for instance, an adolescent girl or a boy may weigh various options of accessing health care for any issue. They may decide that the public health facility is the best option. However, if there are no doctors in the facility or the doctors are unwilling to treat the adolescents without parental consent, then their choice cannot be exercised.

Policies, programmes, and various interventions constitute the opportunity structure for the adolescents. Although facilitative, they fall substantially short of providing enabling opportunities. Thus, they constrain the agency. Significant gaps are evident between the intent, as reflected in the reports of the working groups and the commitments in the policy and programmes, on the one hand and the implementation of these commitments in reality on the other.

Three key factors limit the efficacy of policies and programmes as opportunity structure: attitudes, implementation, and coordination.

Attitudes

Although adolescents were recognised as a distinct group with specific needs, this was not reflected in several individual projects and programmes. For example, the reproductive child health (RCH) programme clubbed adolescent girls under the general category of women until 2006. This perception continues to prevail in many other contexts and programmes. Interventions by the women and child development department or the education department mostly continue to be informed by the perception of adolescents as future parents or by the need to prevent them from indulging in risky behaviour.

Official gatekeepers tend to ensure that adolescents are not well informed. There is a belief that deliberate withholding of information is a protective strategy. This is evident even in the public debate on provision of sexuality education to adolescents in schools. Parents, law makers, and educators tend to believe that provision of information could lead the adolescents astray.

For instance, a request to the Committee on Petitions formed to evolve a consensus on the implementation of the adolescent education programme, comprising Rajya Sabha members from various political parties, contended that sex education in schools was against the cultural fabric of our society. The committee concluded that AEP would vitiate the academic environment of schools and cause incalculable damage to impressionable young minds and thereby corrupt the future citizens of our country. It recommended that 'there should be no sex education in schools' (Rajya Sabha Committee on Petitions 2009).

Given this political backlash, AEP has had to compromise on many aspects. For example, although many references are made to sexual relations, what these entail is either never discussed or is discussed in vague terms. Likewise, discussion of contraception is extremely limited. Methods are explained in abstract and technical terms without indicating their pros and cons, how they are employed, or their usefulness in preventing disease.

Many policies formulated at the national level articulate a commitment to adolescents but overlook the fact that young people are not a homogenous group. Often the policies tend to be ambivalent about married and unmarried adolescents.[6] Importantly, they do not outline how the commitments they make are to be operationalised.

The *Adolescent Reproductive and Sexual Health (ARSH) Guidelines, 2006*, as a part of the Reproductive Child Health (RCH) programme, was certainly a significant policy shift in that it was an effort to overcome some of the barriers in the provision of and access to services for adolescents. For one, it specifically brought adolescent boys, especially the unmarried ones, under the ambit of RCH services. Second, it recognised that unmarried adolescents, both girls and boys, may be engaging in pre-marital sex. Third, it recognised that unmarried adolescents may need special attention and hence proposed dedicated clinics for certain services and counselling.

Rashtriya Kishor Swasthya Karyakram (RKSK) too has recognised diverse groups and provided services to all of them.

However, adolescent needs are rarely seen as rights. Commodities or services are provided more with a view to prevent harm, such as an unwanted pregnancy, rather than as a right of the adolescent to access them.

Implementation

Concerns regarding implementation are primarily two: one, the inability of the system to respond, and two, the attitude of the service providers, who are influenced by the social context.

Interventions often address only one slice of the adolescent needs, such as nutrition or menstrual health or life skills, without a comprehensive look. They also tend to be patchy. For instance, RKSK is implemented in a few blocks in a few districts in each state. Even within a given block, it is implemented only in a few locations. This limits the involvement of the health system in both implementation and monitoring phases. It also significantly reduces the outcome.

One of the authors in a recent field visit found that the young persons highlighted stress caused by studies, employment, and relationships with peers, members of the opposite sex and parents. Service providers also acknowledged this. Yet many counsellors engaged by the health system were unable to advise on these aspects. In fact, counselling tended to be merely information giving. Also, privacy and confidentiality of clients were rarely respected. This defeated the very purpose of the programme. Other studies have raised concerns about the quality of training and abilities of service providers.[7]

Often, provision of services or the establishment of clinics for adolescents was influenced more by availability of space and doctors rather than the consideration of whether they would provide better access to the beneficiaries, as the authors have observed in their assessment of ARSH services in nine states (Jejeebhoy and Santhya 2011).[8] This is reflected in the limited use of the health facilities by adolescents.

Many frontline workers are not comfortable talking with young men or providing commodities such as condoms. The school education programme is focussed more on biological and scientific information, rather than the broader issues of sexuality. The family life education or the life skills education often tends to ignore the adolescents' concerns. The information provided therefore is frequently not even remotely relevant to real concerns of the adolescents.

Coordination/Synergy

Multiple programmes address needs of the adolescents. Although each one mentions the need for convergence and synergy, this rarely occurs in practice. Turf issues of individual departments limit the impact of interventions.

For instance, even the age limits of adolescents have been fixed differently under different programmes. The Youth Policy defines adolescents as falling in the age group between 13 and 19 years; Integrated Child Development Services (ICDS) defines adolescent girls as between 11 and 18 years; the Constitution and labour laws consider those under 14 as children; and RCH mentions adolescents as being between 10 and 19 years of age. The Juvenile Justice (Care and Protection) Act 2000 and 2015 and the Protection of Children from Sexual Offences Act, 2012 define all persons up to the age of 18 years as children. Many other initiatives cover the large 10–24 age group of adolescents and youth. These overlaps in definition of children, youth, and adolescents in various programmes and law lead to issues in programme design, implementation, and coordination across sectors, limiting the impact of the various interventions.

Conclusion

Various policies and programmes recognise the needs and rights of adolescents while outlining the structure of opportunities for them. Nonetheless, their impact is limited. Significant gaps exist between intent, implementation, and the lived reality of the adolescents.

As numerous studies reveal, the agency of the adolescents is limited by the prevailing social norms, values, and cultural practices. The efficacy of the opportunity structure, too, despite the good intent, is limited. This has a significant impact on the empowerment of the adolescents, specifically on their ability to exercise their choice to address their needs. The interventions hardly empower them. Consequently, many issues are seldom addressed and continue to persist. The focus continues to be on soft aspects such as menstrual health and not on issues of sexuality and premarital needs of adolescents. Service providers are reluctant to engage in these issues. They are also unable to address concerns of stress and mental health arising from relationships with parents, peers, and members of the opposite sex. Service is emphasised, but not rights and entitlements of the adolescents. Most importantly, programmes tend to work in silos, with poor synergy and impact.

Some of these issues may be tackled by the following suggestions:

1. Consider a common framework for addressing the varied needs of the adolescents. Perhaps even consider a mission for youth/adolescents;
2. In this framework, assign each department/agency specific responsibility to contribute to the common goal to ensure synergy and impact;
3. Voices and views of young persons should inform the development of this framework; and
4. Sustained communication and advocacy should be undertaken to change mindsets to recognise the rights of the adolescents.

Notes

1. www.censusindia.gov.in/.../Adolescents_and_Youth_in_India_Highlights_from_Census 2011
2. Presentation by Anuradha Gupta at the launch of Rashtriya Kishor Swasthya Karyakram, 2017.
3. http://unicef.in/Whatwedo/33/Adolescents-Nutrition
4. National Health Policy 2003; National Health Policy 2017.
5. Planning commission; Twelfth Five-Year Plan (2012–17).
6. For example, the *National Population Policy, 2000* does not clearly specify if it is proposing services for all adolescents or exclusively for married adolescents. While it does not specifically indicate that unmarried adolescents are ineligible to access services, such statements as 'reproductive health services for adolescent girls and boys are especially significant in rural India, where

adolescent marriage and pregnancy are widely prevalent' suggest a certain ambivalence about the extent to which services will be made available to meet the sexual and reproductive health needs of the unmarried adolescents.

7. See International Institute for Population Sciences and Population Council, 2010.
8. ARSH—Mapping and Developing an Operational Framework for Enhanced Access; (mimeo).

References

Adolescence Education Programme, Facilitators' Guide. (2017), URL: http://164.100.130.11:8091/webarsh/Resources%20on%20ARSH/Adolescent%20Education%20Programme%20Facilitators%20Guide.pdf

Guidelines on School Health Programme (2009), URL: http://mdm.nic.in/Files/School%20Health%20Programme/Guidelines_SHP_29TH_JAN_09-FINAL_FINAL.pdf

Jejeebhoy, S.J. and K.G. Santhya (2011), *Sexual and Reproductive Health of Young People in India: A Review Of Policies, Laws and Programmes*, New Delhi: Population Council.

Johnson, L. (2014), 'Rashtriya Kishor Swasthya Karyakram (RKSK)', *Academic Medical Journal of India*, 2(1), [Online web] accessed on 9 November 2017, URL: http://medicaljournal.in/volume2-issue1-feb-2014-58-correspondence-rashtriya-kishor-swasthya-karyakram-rksk/

Mondal, P. (2017), Highlights on National Population Policy, 2000. Your Article Library, [Online: web] accessed on 7 November 2017, URL: http://www.yourarticlelibrary.com/law/highlights-on-national-population-policy-2000-india/31384

Planning Commission (2001), *Working Group on Adolescents*, New Delhi: Planning Commission, pp. 34–5.

Rajya Sabha Committee on Petitions (2009), URL: http://164.100.47.5/newcommittee/reports/EnglishCommittees/Committee%20on%20Petitions/135-A5-Enghlish-petitions.pdf

Ramanathan S. and V. Chakravarthy (2012), ARSH—Mapping and Developing an Operational Framework for Enhanced Access (mimeo).

SABLA. (2017), Wcdodisha.gov.in, [Online: web] accessed on 9 November 2017, URL: http://wcdodisha.gov.in/content/2/53

School Health Programme (2008), Trinitycarefoundation.org, [Online web] accessed on 9 November 2017, URL: http://trinitycarefoundation.org/preventive/school-health-programme

The National Youth Policy (2003) (2015), *National Health Portal of India*, [Online: web] accessed on 8 November 2017, URL: https://www.nhp.gov.in/the-national-youth-policy-2003_pg

World Health Organization (WHO) (2017), *Mental Health Status of Adolescents in South East Asia: Evidence for Action.*

8

Supporting Adolescents' Sexual Health and Rights

Case Study of Jatan Sansthan, Rajsamand District, Rajasthan

Kanchan Mathur

Introduction

Adolescents (age group of 10–19 years) constitute approximately 22.5 per cent of Rajasthan's population. Of this, adolescent girls comprise 47 per cent. Adolescence is a period of transition from childhood to adulthood marked by a significant growth spurt (the second highest after the first year of life), accompanied by hormonal changes and sexual maturation. The onset of adolescence brings not only changes to their bodies but also new vulnerabilities to human rights abuses, particularly in the arena of sexuality, marriage, and childbearing. For adolescent girls, menstruation begins—preparing them for motherhood, which brings its own risks and complications, which they are hesitant to discuss. Adolescence is also a period of psychosocial, cognitive, and behavioural maturation. These are years of experimentation and risk taking, of giving in to negative peer pressure related to substance use and sexual risk taking. Adolescents also face barriers to reproductive health information and care. Besides, those able to find accurate information about their health and rights may be unable to access the services needed to protect their health and ensure well-being. Whether adolescents can achieve their development potential is determined to a large extent by their social environment and economic factors.

Jatan Sansthan located in Railmagra block of Rajsamand district has been supporting adolescents' sexual and reproductive health by providing access to comprehensive education in sexuality and empowering young people to know and exercise their rights—including the right to delay marriage and the right to refuse unwanted sexual advances.

Section I

Background

Jatan Sansthan is a grassroots not-for-profit organisation working with the rural population of the state of Rajasthan in the districts of Rajsamand, Udaipur, Jhalawar, and Bhilwara. These districts are amongst the most backward districts of the state, and Jatan has covered more than 250 villages across various blocks (Railmagra, Mawli, Sarada, Salumbar, Jhadol, Kherwada, Bhindar, Gogunda, Rishabdev, and Gangapur) in these districts.

Since its inception in 2001, Jatan has designed and implemented various initiatives towards improving the social and demographic indicators of the state with special emphasis on youth, women, girls and adolescents, elected representatives, and marginalised communities. Through the years, Jatan has worked on programmes related to health, education, reproductive rights, and violence against women/girls, strengthening women in governance, migrant labour, and livelihood issues. Jatan also actively works towards participation of the larger community, research, and advocacy to ensure long-lasting impact.

Jatan is attempting to empower the youth of Rajasthan in four districts of the state by providing them a platform where they can express their concerns freely. Jatan also makes available information that enables them to seek social and scientific solutions, thereby helping them become agents of change in their communities. Jatan strives to enhance active participation of youth in decision-making, policy formulation, and advocacy across various forums at national and international level. The programmes for youth are implemented through formation of youth groups/clubs and associations as well as through a strong network of youth volunteers. Besides, Jatan is also working to improve the participation of youth in local governance and public services. The organisation has also provided opportunities to young people in the community to design and implement programmes based on their health and development needs.

Jatan works with panchayats, health service providers, the media, as well as the community to create awareness on health rights of women. Jatan is also working with community members and parents to organise residential camps and short-term trainings that focus on vocational skills, awareness regarding social and gender equality issues, and life skills. The scope of its work has also included community issues such as health, education, employment, and participation in democratic and development processes.

Jatan began its work on sexual and reproductive health by spreading awareness in the community on above issues. Jatan has provided opportunities to young people in the community to design and implement programmes based on their health and development needs. Gender discrimination and female foeticide have been key issues of intervention. Every year, Jatan organises public hearings, media workshops, youth competitions, as well as campaigns to sensitise panchayati raj members, students, and the community at large. Capacity building of youth has been another focus area. Jatan has provided a platform for young people to voice their concerns and search for solutions. Jatan provides regular opportunities to young people to participate at both national- and state-level conventions on sexual and reproductive issues and rights.

Violence against women and girls being a major area of work, the organisation has been running the Mahila Suraksha evam Salah Kendra, which is a redressal centre for female victims of violence. The centre provides an environment of security and support to the girls, women, and children victims of violence to enable them to make their own decision about modes of combating violence. Besides counselling, the centre tries to link women and girls with critical services such as legal, psychiatric, referral services, and medical support. It also provides short stay facilities, livelihood support, etc., thus providing a holistic response to a violent situation. The centre undertakes intensive case work, providing emotional support, helping women/girls to analyse their situation, counselling them for positive change and mediating with the perpetrators of violence.

Section II

Project Hilor

In 2012, Jatan began focussing on empowering marginalised communities with special emphasis on geographical areas where girls often drop out of school or never attend one, are forced into marriage at an early age or coerced into sexual relations, trafficked, and exploited.

Hilor (also known as Action for Adolescent Girls—AAG) is a comprehensive strategy to empower adolescent girls in two identified blocks of Udaipur district of Rajasthan through a framework of building social, health, and economic assets to enable adolescent girls to protect their human rights. Taking cognizance of the needs of the out-of-school adolescent girls, Hilor addresses the complex issues of early marriage, school dropouts, skill empowerment, and social consciousness through a strategic approach of asset building in the area of social, health/reproductive health, and financial literacy.

The project's key objectives include enhancing adolescent girl's skills and perspectives on gender and social equity issues, improve their access to health information and services, and provide opportunities for continued education and linkages with appropriate work opportunities. On a broader level, the project aims to create, orient, and support a sensitised, robust, and effective network of adolescent peer educators: the grassroots functionaries for empowering the adolescent girls to realise their aspirations and also develop an enabling environment through effective partnerships with various community-level entities such as gram panchayat, government, and local civil society organisations.

The implementation of the project is being carried out through the non-nutritional component of the large-scale SABLA initiative of the Directorate of Women's Empowerment, Government of Rajasthan. The programme is rolled out in the field through implementing partners/non-governmental organisations (NGOs) working in the area of youth and women's empowerment. The technical and financial support is provided by UNFPA under its global initiative, AAG, which aims to invest in scale up evidence-based and targeted interventions to reach the most vulnerable adolescent girls in 12 countries including India with high rates of child marriage over the next 5 years.

Girl-Centric Curriculum Development

The AAG initiative is being implemented by Jatan in two blocks (Kherwada and Salumber) of Udaipur district through anganwadi centres and Accredited Social Health Activists (ASHAs) since 2014. The choice of the districts was made looking at the fact that within Rajasthan, Udaipur is one district that has 80 per cent tribal population and 47 per cent population living below poverty line. Out of 12 blocks in Udaipur district, Kherwara block with predominantly tribal population of 74 per cent has a sex ratio of 964 women per 1,000 men and a child sex ratio of 916 girls per 1,000 boys.

Schedule tribes do not own much land although most of them are involved in agriculture-related work. Seasonal migration is prominent in this area, and people generally migrate to Gujarat to work in cotton farming, construction, and other services. Many children and adolescents, especially girls, migrate to work in the BT (*Bacillus Thuringiensis*) cotton fields. Thus, they lack other acquired occupational skills and vocational training. Adolescents, especially girls, are denied the investments and opportunities that they need to realise their full potential. Often they are not valued, and opportunities for their development are compromised at all stages of life. This cycle of neglect manifests through discrimination in educational opportunities, gender-based violence, and harmful practices, such as gender-biased sex selection, early marriage, and dowry.

The need for Hilor initiative was imperative looking at the above situation. Hilor attempts to deliver life skills, linkages to formal/non-formal education, vocational skills, training, knowledge of existing public services, promote spacing and care seeking behaviour for sexual and reproductive health, and increase median age at birth among married adolescent girls 15–19 years of age. The programme has been rolled out through collectivisation of adolescent girls and transaction of life skills; it also engages with parents and community members, frontline workers, and local administrative officials. The initiative aims to protect girls' human rights through a combination of targeted interventions that delay age at marriage and childbearing, prevent unintended pregnancy, and enhance health, social, and economic assets among the most vulnerable girls. The effort is to foster a successful transition into productive and rewarding adulthood for its current generation of young people.

Guided by the national priorities and its global mandate, the AAG initiative works across a continuum of life transitions from unmarried to married adolescent girls with investments in existing government programmes so that gains consolidated in the project can be sustained and the initiative can be replicated in other geographies with relevant adaptations to the local context.

Rationale for the Development of a Girl-Centric Curriculum

The overall design of the AAG initiative aims to work with girl groups through adolescent peer educators who are supported by the project staff. A girl-centric curriculum that is well-designed and transacted by neo-literate peer educators and is aligned with local realities is hence an important priority for this initiative.

While developing the curriculum, the responsiveness of the materials to the local context and participatory nature of the activities were emphasised. Another aspect kept in mind was having enhanced opportunities for reinforcement of learning.

Guiding Principles, Process, and Design: The 4As Framework

Using the 4As organising framework, the curriculum aims to develop life skills to enable girls to respond to real-life situations effectively. The 4As framework is based on the premise that every individual has an experience or information that connects her/him to a specific theme, and that the curriculum needs to establish that connection between the learner and curriculum. This is the purpose of the anchor in the framework, who builds on the existing knowledge, beliefs, and experiences of learners through engaging narratives or brainstorming in small groups or plenary formats. This is followed by add, which provides an opportunity to introduce a new concept, idea, tool, or resource to the learners and comprises the teachable moment of the curriculum. This is followed by apply, which encourages learners to link their own experience to the new learning and then apply it to deal with an existing situation or challenge. The away section links the learning to real-life situations of learners so that the learning is reinforced and anchored in the experiences of the learners. It also provides opportunities for linking different sections of the curriculum.

Training is imparted on the basis of the 'Peer-educators' module. The module of the Hilor project uses a girl-centric approach for the comprehensive development of adolescent girls to realise their aspirations. With the overall goal of empowering girls by enhancing their health and social and economic assets, the curriculum is delivered in a phased manner. The entire curriculum package consists of 26 meetings organised once every fortnight at the Girls Clubs that meet at the anganwadi centres in the villages within project geographies. Based on the experience of peer-led curriculum transactions and due to the sensitivity and complexity of some themes, certain sessions are pre-selected for transaction or co-facilitated by an adult mentor.

Additional meetings are also organised for older adolescents in the age group of 15–19 years, keeping in mind their experience appropriateness and cultural sensitivities. The curriculum is learner led and focusses on learning by doing. Hence, in effect the objective of the curriculum is an enhancement of skills rather than transfer of knowledge. The peer educators (facilitators) and learners enter a partnership where everyone is learning together and every individual takes the responsibility for her learning without establishing hierarchies.

The key themes addressed in the curriculum include the following:

1. Getting to know one another, learning to express oneself in group settings, and listen to one another.
2. Improved understanding of self:
   (i) Improved understanding of one's personality; and
   (ii) Understanding personal and social identities with special focus on the realities of being a girl.
3. Working in teams:
   (i) Enhancing skills to problem solving and help one another;
   (ii) Developing an understanding of adolescent girls group as a support group; and
   (iii) Effective ways of working in groups.
4. Relationships:
   (i) Appreciation of attributes of positive (healthy and nurturing) and negative (exploitative) relationships;
   (ii) Effective communication skills; and
   (iii) Skills for nurturing positive relationships and getting out of negative relationships (ability to take decisions and refuse exploitation).
5. Enhanced understanding of health and well-being:
   (i) Nutrition and balanced diet;
   (ii) Prevention of anaemia; and

   (iii) Hygienic practices associated with cooking, storing, and eating.

6. Understanding and managing emotions.
7. Changes during adolescence:
   (i) Physical, emotional, and psychological changes and being comfortable with them;
   (ii) What does it mean to experience adolescence: body image, feelings of attraction? and
   (iii) Menstruation: What is it, menstrual hygiene, challenging social taboos related to menstruation.
8. Child marriage: causes, consequences, and putting a stop to it.
9. Responsible sex behaviour including information and access to contraceptives and reproductive rights.
10. Gender, its construction in our society, and implications for adolescent girls:
    (i) To build an understanding on gender and sexuality, including roles, stereotypes and diversity;
    (ii) To clarify myths related to gender and sexuality;
    (iii) Understanding of influence of gender on the opportunities for girls; and
    (iv) Recognising and challenging stereotypes.
11. Gender-based Violence (GBV):
    (i) To understand the nature of discrimination, harassment, and violation.
    (ii) Where do incidents of GBV occur? and
    (iii) What can be done to prevent, report, and manage these incidents:
        (a) To be able to communicate feelings of and experiences of violation;
        (b) To develop confidence to protect oneself and stand up for one another; and

(c) Rights of adolescent girls in institutions such as the police stations.

12. Financial literacy:
    (i) Identify and map earnings and expenses;
    (ii) Concept of savings and skills to plan for goal-based savings;
    (iii) Options for borrowing money and responsibilities associated with borrowing money; and
    (iv) Financial institutions for saving money and taking loans.

Cluster Meetings

Cluster meetings are conducted once in a month at each cluster (25 clusters in total) in which all the peer educators participate. The main objectives of the cluster meetings is (a) to help form adolescent girls understanding on a new topic from the Module and (b) to share their experience and learning of the previous adolescents meeting that they had conducted in their respective adolescent clubs.

The *Sakhi and Sahelis'* trainings (meetings of peer educators) are conducted to build an understanding on topics related to facilitation skills, sexual rights and behaviour, gender, violence, sexually transmitted diseases, importance of money loaning, and financial management among adolescent girls. The entire workshop is based on the participatory mode of training in which games and fun activities become an integral part of the module. The Sakhi and Saheli meetings were conducted over the entire duration of 2016 starting from the month of January to December 2016. Eighty per cent of the peer educators participated in the meetings on an average; as the peer educators are leaders, it is their responsibility to participate in these meetings. Through participation in cluster meetings, they also got an opportunity to move out of their homes, which gives them greater spatial mobility and freedom.

Adolescent Girls Meeting

Fortnightly adolescent meetings are conducted by peer educators in their respective adolescent clubs with the help and support of anganwadi workers (AWWs) and cluster coordinators under the Hilor project. The meetings provide the participants an opportunity to discuss with the resource persons difficulties faced by them while discussing topics such as menstruation and sexual behaviour and what can be done to overcome the challenges.

In the initial stages, the parents were hesitant to allow their girls to attend the meeting on their own. Hence, the cluster coordinator had to visit the house of each and every adolescent girl before conducting a meeting. The same cluster coordinators conduct the training as a resource person resulting in a synergy between the two and a positive outcome.

Use of the Resource Materials

A common understanding was developed on the principles of the curriculum and work within the 4As framework through a series of workshops which helped evolve theme-based resource materials organised in the form of meetings that had to be conducted in fortnightly sessions with adolescent girl groups.

To make the implementation process more sustainable, the peer educators were given training on various life skills related to health and cultural and social issues in a form of designed module, which is broken down in 26 meetings, and each meeting deals with a different aspects of development of the adolescent girls' life. These peer educators in turn train their village adolescent groups. The adolescent peer educators are oriented on the content and use of these resource materials in phased residential trainings. Each training is of 4–5 days' duration and has two distinct components: (a) orienting peer educators on the content of the meetings and (b) preparing peer educators to transact the meetings in the presence of trainers who provide specific guidance and support to the peer educators on the delivery of content, facilitation skills, time management, and engaging their audience.

This strategy provides the necessary clarity to the peer educators on their role in transacting the meetings. The importance of prior preparation in conducting meetings effectively is emphasised. In the meetings assigned to the adult mentors, the supportive role of peer educators is clearly specified. The curriculum is transacted by investing in orientation of the senior project staff through master trainers. The senior staff members then orient the adult mentors. The curriculum is hence a combination of master trainers, senior project staff, and adult mentors orienting the peer educators.

Learning and Challenges

Some challenges confronting Jatan Sansthan in implementing the Hilor project are related to peer educators leaving the group due to various reasons such as early marriage, migration to Gujarat, and daily wage work. Peer educators are therefore unable to participate in the cluster meetings. In Kherwara block particularly, if girls are not in school or continuing their education in any form, they are most likely to get married before 18 years or migrate for work. To avoid this, special measures were adopted to enrol the out-of-school peer educators to schools or in some vocation skill course.

Some of the anganwadi centres are difficult to access, and peer educators of these areas find travelling to them difficult. In those villages, if the ASHA and AWWs are occupied with their department work, there is absenteeism of peer educators. To deal with this situation, a list of such AWWs is prepared, and the cluster coordinators prepare a micro plan with the AWW of these areas for their travel so that the participation of the peer educators could be ensured.

To increase the participation of the peer educators who work as daily wage workers, the field team interacted with the local employers and persuaded them to give a 2-hour break to the adolescent girls so that they could come for the meetings. Many employers gave their consent, whereas others did not agree.

Many peer educators found it difficult to take sessions. According to them, as most of the adolescent girls coming to the meeting are non-school going, they feel very uncomfortable to speak in front of them as they feel that the girls might make fun of them. To solve this issue, the team encouraged the other adolescent club members also to take sessions with the peer educators by pairing them up so as to increase each other's confidence.

The issues around menstruation, child marriage, and physical changes often make the girls uncomfortable. In some villages, the parents also raise an objection on the content of the meetings and do not allow their girls to participate in them. Their participation was increased to some extent due to regular visits by cluster coordinators to the homes of girls and counselling them during parent meetings.

Issues around sexual behaviour, sexually transmitted diseases, and gender-based violence and related issues are generally not discussed on a day-to-day basis due to the many social and cultural taboos attached to them. However, over time, efforts have been made to encourage the peer educators, and many of them have begun discussing issues openly. Hence, once the space is created for adolescent girls to discuss these topics, primarily in the local language with known people, who in this case is the cluster coordinator with whom they have a good rapport, they discuss such topics more freely and also share their own experiences on the same.

Impact of the Project

1. Since 2015, project Hilor has made a significant impact on the lives of adolescent girls in Kherwara block.
2. The project has succeeded in creating a platform for adolescent girls to discuss and share experiences. It has enhanced their understanding on rights and taking decisions regarding age at marriage. It has succeeded in facilitating open and frank discussion around issues hitherto not discussed such as menstruation, menstrual

hygiene management, and sexual and reproductive health and rights.

3. Adolescent girls have been imparted skill and livelihood development training in tailoring, beautician courses, and mobile repair, which have opened up avenues for work. Adolescent girls have also been encouraged to seek employment in organisations such as Big Bazaar and in nearby factories.
4. Several dropout girls have enrolled in Standard X and XII through the National Open Schooling Scheme.
5. The project has inculcated a habit of saving through formation of Self-Help Group (SHGs). Girls now have begun saving ₹ 50 per month and depositing in the local post office. Financial literacy regarding functioning of banks and post offices is also provided.
6. Adolescent girls' understanding on gender-based violence has been strengthened, and they are now raising voice on issues of gender equality.
7. Several girls have emerged as leaders and represented the organisation at the state and national level. One girl represented Jatan at an international forum.
8. Girls have begun submitting proposals to the gram sabha for construction of roads and toilets and provision of regular electricity supply.
9. There is an enhanced understanding regarding health, nutrition, and hygiene among the girls covered by the project.
10. AWWs and ASHAs have begun transacting Life Skills Education (LSE) and discussing issues around menstruation and sexuality.
11. There is a reduction in child marriages in Kherwara block, increase in age at marriage, and ability to make informed choices regarding marriage.

Section III

Addressing Reproductive and Menstrual Health

Jatan Sansthan and Vikalp (a design studio) collaborated on reproductive and menstrual health work in rural areas of south Rajasthan, India. Their continued outreach in the field and research over these past 15 years has brought to light many issues around the area of menstruation and menstrual hygiene management.

Beliefs and practices around menstruation affect a women's self-image and self-esteem, her health and well-being, and her position in the society. In resource-poor communities, cloth from old garments and other rags continues to be methods used to manage menstrual flow. While cloth in itself is not unhygienic, there are many negative practices around managing menstrual cloth that can potentially cause infections. For example the cloth needs to be dried in the sun to sterilise it, but this may not be done due to the shame and stigma attached. With these cultural and other reasons, a strong need was felt to create awareness about menstrual hygiene management and the need for creation of a socially acceptable, affordable, and safe menstrual product.

About Uger Project

The Uger Project was initiated in 2011. 'Uger', meaning 'new beginnings' in Mewari language of south Rajasthan, is a movement focussing on breaking the silence around menstruation and promoting menstrual health.

1. It combats the growing use of disposable menstrual products and bringing back respect to reuse. This has been done by the design and development of *Uger* reusable cloth pads.
2. It helps a women's group to earn a supplementary income for their families by stitching.
3. It includes men in menstruation, who are otherwise marginalised.

4. It helps women perceive and talk about and manage menstruation positively, connecting with their bodies to make healthy choices and care for the environment.

The *Uger* project has four well-defined areas of work. All Uger products go through rigorous research. Uger has been put through 'cross over product studies' and its sustainability has been established, from the environment, economic, social, and health perspectives.

1. *Environment*: The products decompose within 4–6 months as they are made of cotton cloth, a natural fabric. This causes no negative environmental impact.
2. *Health:* Products cause no allergies, no itching, boils, and abscesses.
3. *Economic:* Priced at ₹ 720 (prices may vary) for a pack of six pads, it can be reused over 1.5 years. For women who cannot afford these expenses, the project provides guidance on how to stitch the pads.
4. *Social:* The product provides dignity, giving the philosophy of 'no waste' and 'reuse' a space, which is urgently required in the current contexts of 'use and throw'.

Jatan Sansthan conducts regular training programmes for young people, both men and women, across different communities and demographics to sensitise them to all aspects of menstruation and management. Health educators are also trained. Several collaborative workshops have been organised with the Greater Mumbai Municipal Corporation Mumbai, Spark Minda Foundation Pune, Pantnagar and Chennai, Urmul Setu Trust—Bikaner, Conservation Wild lands Pench, Plan India Jaipur, and other organisations in Bihar and Jharkhand.

The products are sold at the Jatan centre and on different online portals. Jatan has also developed reusable cloth diapers as of August of 2017 for newborns, infants, and children. These products have been researched and field tested and are available at the centre. These are available in three sizes: 0–6 months, 6–12 months, and 1–2 years.

Impact of Uger Project Over the Past 3 Years

The project has led to women's empowerment by breaking the silence around menstrual health and management (MHM; https://ugerpads.jimdo.com/; http://www.jatansansthan.org/areaofwork/safe-menstrual-health-uger/). It has encouraged advocacy and partnerships with state governments, Corporate Social Responsibility (CSR), UN agencies, institutional donors, and civil society organisations. The project has grown and expanded through knowledge building and creation of replicable models from one state to seven states of India; trainings have been organised on MHM for various stakeholders in rural and urban contexts. Over 3,000 stakeholders have been covered directly through these trainings in the past 3 years. The project has led to reduction of menstrual debris into landfills. Approximately 300 women and girls from urban areas have shifted to using reusable cloth pads from disposables. The project has also led to income augmentation through enterprise for women who are trained to stitch cloth pads.

Advocacy work with male members in decision-making positions of several departments such as health and Department of Women's Empowerment and involving district collectors, college and school staff, and members of civil society organisations has been initiated.

Five male members have been inducted as part of the Uger trainer's team. They have taken up the task of conducting MHM trainings with women, girls, and boys in rural and urban contexts, breaking several social barriers and stereotypes. Over 300 boys and men have been trained (150 directly and 150 indirectly) on various aspects of women's health rights and increasing their participation in menstrual management. Trainings have also been conducted with over 2,000 rural women and girls on various aspects of MHM.

Around 400 women and girls have been trained to stitching their own cloth pads for personal use and economic benefit through local sales. Creating spaces for discussions on sustainable menstrual management practices through participation in government-organised melas and sale/distribution of subsidised cloth pads. More than 3,000 women and girls have been covered.

The urban upper middle class audience, who are privileged with access to information and luxury of making choices, have been an important target audience for Uger. Uger has actively promoted reusable cloth pads as a healthy and eco-friendly option. Approximately 300 women have shifted to using Uger pads from disposable options, thus reducing non-biodegradable waste going to landfills. Using Facebook, online sale options, and urban melas (fairs) as a tool to discuss the issue and promote reusable pads. More than 500 urban women and men have purchased these pads for themselves and others. Sale of pads has led to the economic augmentation of the five women associated with the Uger self-help group in the past 3 years coming from the slum areas of Udaipur, Rajasthan involved in pad stitching. They earn an average of ₹ 4,000 per month. Sale of pads has also helped the project attain partial financial sustainability.

The project has nurtured a team of male and female trainers (eight female + five male trainers) on MHM who can conduct 1-day- to 3-day-long trainings on menstrual health and pad making in rural and urban contexts.

Section IV

Conclusion

What lessons can be drawn from the case study of Jatan Sansthan? What is the possibility of replicating the two projects initiated by the organisation? It is envisaged that the learning of the AAG initiative will be scaled up through the SABLA programme in the state and in other states. Also, ASHAs cater to married adolescent girls 15–19 years to increase mean age at first conception, median age at first birth, promote spacing between two pregnancies, and care-seeking behaviour for sexual and reproductive health. By embracing the above strategy from both the programmes, adolescent clubs are formed at anganwadi centres. Each group is led by three peer educators and a cluster coordinator from the project. The group is supported by ASHA and AWW at the village level. The group meets on a fortnightly basis to discuss various issues related to the life skills, health, and social and cultural topics. The mandate of AAG is simple, and the programme is already being implemented in one block (Gumma) of Gajapati district in Odisha since 2014. Within Rajasthan, Centre for Community Economics and Development Consultants Society (CECOEDECON), an NGO has adopted the mandate of AAG and is implementing the project through the *Beti Bachao Beti Padao* programme with UNFPA support in in four districts. There is hence immense possibility of replicating the AAG initiative throughout the country through anganwadi centres and ASHAs.

Uger project, 3 years ago, in 2014, it was on the verge of shutting down with no funds to sustain and was being kept alive on Jatan's corpus fund operating locally in and around Udaipur. Today, it has expanded to seven states of India with partnerships with state governments such as Governments of Bihar, Maharashtra, Jharkhand, and Rajasthan, institutional donors, and CSRs; UNFPA Delhi, Jaipur; Plan India International; Spark Minda Foundation; and Tata water mission. Replicable training modules on MHM and pad stitching have already been created and can be adopted by trainers across geographies.

References

Annual Report (2015), 'Action for Adolescent Girls, Intervention Area Kherwara Block, Implemented by Jatan Sansthan, Jatan Sansthan, Udaipur'.

Annual Report (2016), 'Hilor Project, Intervention Area Kherwara Block, Implemented by Jatan Sansthan, Jatan Sansthan, Udaipur'.

Annual Report Spark Minda foundation (2016), 'Uger Project Partners with for Spark Minda Foundation for Trainings', New Delhi, pp. 30–35, 72.

Murthy, L. 'Project Uger', [Online web], URL: http://krya.in/blogk/2014/07/a-new-beginning-conversations-with-ugers-lakshmi-murthy/

9

Empowering Adolescent Girls

Case Study of Adolescent Girls' Camps of Ajit Foundation

Jayshree Godara*

Introduction

A thorough understanding of adolescence in society calls for multi-pronged perspectives—one that includes psychology, biology, history, sociology, education, and anthropology. However, from all these angles, adolescence is viewed as a transitional period between childhood and adulthood, and that major objective of development of adolescents is to prepare them for the adult role. It is recognised as a period of multiple transitions: in education, health, livelihood, and social relations. As a result, several concerns need to be addressed. These include behavioural and psychological issues, educational issues, and health issues. Among these, generally greater attention is given to physical health, as neglecting this aspect may result in risky behaviour, pregnancy, and infectious diseases.

Indian policymakers have recognised the potential of adolescents and have made efforts to harness their strength for

* With inputs from V.S. Vyas and Jyotsana Rajvanshi.

development. Since the early 1980s, the government focussed on population control and education to enable young people to make socially responsible choices. Apart from stand-alone programmes and schemes, these concerns were made an integral part of the educational system. Teachers and parents were to be important players of these initiatives. The objective was to provide knowledge and information that would lead to self-confidence and self-reliance among adolescents and enable them to face the realities of life. These efforts became more focussed on girls with the announcement of Decade of the Girl Child (1991–2000).

Adolescence, particularly in the girls' life, is a very critical stage. Within a short period, rapid developments take place in their physiology. Also mental and emotional processes undergo remarkable changes. Because information on such topics is not easily accessible, girls find it difficult to handle the changes both physically and psychologically. Our social system does not provide an open forum to discuss these issues. As a result, the girls are misinformed and develop several inhibitions and complexes, more so in a tradition-bound society such as that of Rajasthan. In such societies, not only open discussion on the problems of adolescent girls is discouraged but also efforts to acquire relevant knowledge through different sources are also frowned upon.

Adolescents have a keen sense of inquisitiveness and have abundant energy. In the absence of proper outlets, they get confused. Several distortions take place in their behaviour, in inter-personal relationships, and in their understanding of society at large. It is necessary to appreciate the questions arising in their minds and help them address them by facilitating healthy solutions. As a result of lack of participation by adolescents and youth in policy and programmes, many vital issues affecting them are overlooked. There is a need to prioritise efforts to prepare adolescents to shoulder challenging responsibilities.

There is a consensus among educationists and development activists that education, among other things, could be used to bring about a fundamental change in the lives of the adolescents. The Ministry of Human Resource Development, recognising the importance of education, invests in several initiatives and partnerships to create and strengthen opportunities for young people to select better life options. There are few other important government programmes aimed at the betterment of adolescents. We may mention two among the more important ones.

The Rajiv Gandhi Scheme for Empowerment of Adolescent Girls or Sabla is a centrally sponsored programme of Government of India initiated in 2011 by the Ministry of Women and Child Development. Rashtriya Kishor Swasthya Karyakram of the Ministry of Health and Family Welfare is a health programme for adolescents in the age group of 10–19 years. It aims for awareness regarding improved nutrition, reproductive health, substance abuse, among other objectives. Similarly, Saathiya resource kit was launched in villages with the objective of connecting nearly 26 crore youth. These and several other initiatives have been examined in the papers included in this book.

Ajit Foundation

The *Ajit Foundation* was established in the year 1994 with a focus on youth development. It is a voluntary organisation working in the walled city of Bikaner in Rajasthan. Vision of the foundation is 'Empowered Youth: Enlightened Citizens' its mission is to provide 'Space for Creativity: Inculcate Sense of Responsibility'. It is working with young people, helping them to learn, explore, and enquire, and providing spaces that nurture creativity and foster a sense of social responsibility.

The vision, mission, and objectives of *Ajit Foundation* are particularly noteworthy as it is functioning in the context of a traditional society that has not recognised the specific needs of adolescents and young people. In such societies, due to early marriage and associated cultural practices, childhood transforms directly into adulthood. The enabling social environment required to understand and address the needs of adolescents does not exist. It is in this specific context that the foundation began its activities.

It is trying to achieve its objectives through the following interventions, which may be called its core areas of work: (a) community resource centre, (b) dialogue series, (c) community libraries, (d) scientific resource centre, and (e) workshops, trainings, and camps for capacity building of adolescents and youths. A brief description of these activities follows.

The Community Resource Centre includes a library that stocks around 18,000 books and subscribes/receives nearly 40 periodicals. It has audio-visual equipment and a number of multimedia items. It attracts a large number of users. A few of them are regular users, and some visit the library for specific requirement, i.e. preparing for various examinations. The use of the library for reading and consultation is free and open for all. There is a token membership fee that is charged only for those who borrow books to take home. At present, there are nearly 300 members of the library, and around 30–40 youth visit every day. The Community Resource Centre encourages young boys and girls to form interest groups in the area of science, environment, history, and literature. It also provides a space for young people to interact, discuss, and share their thoughts in a free environment.

As an extension of the main library of the Community Research Centre, to bring in more readers and participants from the outlying *mohallas*, community/*mohalla* libraries have been established in the government primary schools. These are located in eight *mohallas*. Each library is given about 300 books, three to four magazines, a newspaper and a set of toys. Children and adolescents from the neighbourhood use these libraries. Prior to the establishment of community or *mohalla* libraries, the foundation had started *tonga library* that carried a small number of books and magazines in a horse-drawn cart and went to different *mohallas* at fixed timings on fixed days of the week, enabling the young people in these *mohallas* to use the library services. On popular demand from the *mohalla*, local libraries were established. These libraries are managed by women or school- and college-going youth of the *mohalla*.

The *mohalla* libraries by turn produce Hindi magazine, *Chahal-Pahal*. It is handwritten with beautiful artwork.

The foundation also brings out a monthly magazine in Hindi called *Vikalp*. To a large extent, the contents of this magazine are developed by young writers. It includes essays, poetry, stories, and opinion pieces and covers the wide range of issues that have relevance to sociocultural and economic aspects. The magazine is in the 15th year of its uninterrupted publications.

Under the Dialogue Series, the foundation invites a number of speakers from diverse field, politics, fine arts, literature, philosophy, and all names to reckon with in their own field and have exemplified human values. The series creates a platform for the young people to listen to and interact with great minds. Over the years, more than 40 leaders in their respective fields have addressed the youth.

Workshops, trainings, and educational visits are organised for capacity building of adolescents and youths. In the summer and winter vacations, a numbers of such workshops and training sessions are organised to meet the objective of youth development. In these events, youth discuss their problems and also organise constructive activities, mostly on their own initiative but with support from well-informed and knowledgeable adults. A number of training workshops are being held for boys and girls on a wide range of subjects such as career counselling, science, kitchen gardening, *mehendi*, flower making, best from waste, theatre, sculpture, computers and internet, music, and yoga.

An annual chess competition for school boys from the city and adjoining areas has become an excellent platform for bonding and interaction. About 30–40 teams (three chess players in each team) participate in this annual competition, which is now in its 10th year.

Adolescent Girls' Camps

Adolescent girl's camps are a non-residential 4-day event to empower girls and prepare them for their future life. These camps are aimed to impart essential knowledge on health, nutrition, education, social relations, rights, and responsibilities. These camps were made non-residential because it was difficult to persuade parents to allow girls to stay overnight. Details of genesis of the Adolescent Girls Empowerment Camps and the description of earlier camps are narrated by Jyotsana Rajvanshi in the report, 'Fragrance of life: Awareness and Capacity Building Programs for Adolescent in Bikaner'. In these camps, specialists from different fields impart relevant knowledge. Practical training is given to the participants to build confidence and to empower them.

Primarily three aspects of learning were emphasised in these camps:

1. Educational aspects;
2. Behavioural aspects; and
3. Exposure visits.

The main theme on which training takes place are:

1. Physical and psychological changes occurring with the onset of adolescence;
2. Nutritional needs of adolescents;
3. Women's empowerment through education and law;
4. Challenges faced by women; and
5. 'Positive Thinking'.

Although training covers a wide range of topics, the final aim is to encourage young women to understand themselves and the world they live in, which is identified with the prevailing social mores and gender bias.

The idea of conducting camps was born out of the realisation that adolescent girls are imparted very little knowledge about their body by any person in their family or outside. While it is a culturally accepted norm that only mothers discuss such sensitive topics with their daughters, in many cases even they give only minimum knowledge. The purpose of such advice is generally to prepare the girls to face their menstrual periods. This is but a small step in making the girls fully prepared for the new phase of life they are entering. This was the primary objective with which the camps started. Later on, other aspects were added to the contents of trainings. In the earlier years, these camps were held thrice a year, and more recently, these are organised twice a year and generally are organised during holidays, either during summer vacation or around Christmas or *Dussahra—Diwali* break.

Each camp admits on an average of 20–30 participants, usually in the age range of 10–20 years. The girls belong to both Hindu and Muslim communities; they come from different castes and mainly from the *mohallas* in the walled city. The number of girls from different communities has varied from one camp to another. During one year, camps were held for adolescent boys and girls together; in another camp, mothers or elderly ladies from the families of the participants were also invited. At the start, the participants are told about the history of *Ajit Foundation* and its vision and mission. The objectives of the camps are explained and the importance of the training is emphasised. Resource persons in camps are specialists in their subjects. They include medical doctors, nutritionists, women activists, judges, psychologists, and career counsellors.

The key issues that are discussed in these camps briefly, are described.

Adolescence: A Transitional Phase

The meaning of adolescence as a transition between childhood and adulthood is discussed with participants, as it encompasses a number of physical, physiological, emotional, mental, and psychological changes. Girls are informed that any period of life tends to be characterised by certain developments but a number of significant characteristics make this phase of life distinct from all other phases. They have to learn to accept these changes and come to terms with them.

Social Issues

Prevalent social issues that are responsible for the status of women and girls are discussed in these camps. It was noted that early marriage, early pregnancy, inadequate nutrition intake, myths, and superstitions are the issues that the participants want to discuss. Suggestions to overcome these challenges are given by the resource persons.

Reproductive Health and Hygiene and Pathological/ Clinical Examination

The issues of the girl child are raised in these camps keeping health the main focus. To know their health status, experts from College of Home Science check weight, height, and haemoglobin of participants and discuss their medical findings with them. A common feature is that girls are below the approved haemoglobin level, and are underweight for their age.

The girls are familiarised to the concept of reproductive health, its meaning and importance, and sexually imparted diseases, what they are and how to prevent them and what treatments become necessary. Girls are informed about various factors related to personal hygiene, menstrual hygiene, and management of menstrual problems. A gynaecologist lectures about the menstrual cycle and problems during menstruations and suggests possible solutions. She explains about the infection in the genital organs and their symptoms and causes. In these sessions, the importance of cleanliness and hygienic conditions in the surroundings is greatly emphasised. This session proves to be extremely well accepted. The girls do not hesitate in asking questions that may have haunted them for long.

Balanced Food Intake

In this session, causes of anaemia are explained. The girls are informed that anaemia is caused due to lack of iron, lack of vitamin B12, lack of folic acid, excessive loss of blood during menstruation, etc., also due to infection in stomach or intestine and smoking.

The nutrition problems affecting the participants are discussed with them in the session. Deliberations held and advice given on their daily food consumption pattern, and they are informed about nutrients, micro-nutrients, vitamins, proteins, and their importance in a balanced diet. Reasons of malnutrition and obesity are discussed. The dietary planning and prevention of anaemia are explained. The consumption of green salad and vegetables and fruits rich in calcium, vitamin A, B, E, and C, iron, and beta-carotene is emphasised. Girls actively participate in this session.

Confidence Building and Communication

The special needs of the girl child, especially those related to her emotional needs and the traumas of growing up as a subordinate person in society, are focussed upon and discussed in detail.

Laws and Rights of Women

Resource persons make participants aware of the challenges faced by women while doing any type of work. The sessions cover the laws and discuss live case studies. Advocate and legal experts hold this session. They also tell them about their duties such as fighting evil social customs, ensuring security of public property, saying 'no' to discrimination, and awareness towards environment. They are given information on women's welfare laws, forums for raising voice against domestic violence and sexual harassment, right to equality ensured by the Constitution, prohibition of gender decimations, free education till the age of 14, and child marriage restrain act.

Role Play and Case Studies

Girls are encouraged to take up a role in play on the issues of dowry system, domestic violence, education, foeticide, etc. *Seema Ki Samasya*, a case study on frustrations of teenage girls of small cities and protective families, was discussed in one of the camps.

During this session, there is live wire excitement amongst the attendees. They all use their creative ideas to prepare the script of the play within a limited time and also perform their role convincingly. The topics on which role plays are prepared are very sensitive and at the same time very important.

The importance of freedom of self-expression/assertiveness and other relevant topics are discussed. Films such as *Honhar Bachche, Meena, Thoda Sa Romani Ho Jaaye, Koi Mil Gaya,* and *Angur* were exhibited in different camps.

Educational Visits

On the fourth and last day of the camp, girls are taken to places that could have importance in their life and career. For example, there are taken to a court, where they learn about the work done in the courts; college of Home Science, where teachers explain the importance and scope of Home Science as a subject; or radio and television stations, where the concerned officials delve on the working of radio and television. An important part of this programme is a visit to women police station, where they are informed about the laws related to women and also given the helpline number, which could be used in case of emergency.

During some camps, girls were taken outside of Bikaner. For example, occasional field visits to non-governmental organisations, such as Urmul and Doosra Dashak, were organised. On another occasion, girls went in a group to a numbers of places, such as Nagaur, Ajmer, Udaipur, Mount Abu, and Jodhpur, for sightseeing. A written permission is sought from the parents prior to the inclusion of the girls in an outstation camp.

New Activities Added

In the beginning of a camp, group songs and *Masti Ki Pathshala* are organised to act as ice breakers.

In the course of the camp, career counselling is done for the interested participants.

Another innovation in recent camps was to invite the mothers of teenage girls. They were counselled about the ways to manage adolescent girls and boys. They are advised to be a good friend of their child, be non-judgmental, create confidence, allow adolescents to take decisions, and encourage them to raise voice against evil customs. The outcome of this initiative was indeed heartening.

Impact of the Programme on the Participants

These camps helped the girls to gain self-confidence and also provided substantive knowledge. It was observed that there is remarkable improvement in the level of self-confidence and capacity of articulation among the girls. With the passage of time, even the body language of the girls underwent a change—the attendees started looking up and making eye contact with each other and even with the resource persons!

Girls who participated in these camps have shown a desire to be gainfully employed to become independent. They also dream about interesting careers that challenge gender stereotypes. For example, some of the girls desired to join the police force. One girl even wanted to be a pilot, though she could not pursue her ambition. A few have taken up teaching jobs or other government jobs or are attempting to join Rajasthan Administrative Services. A major accomplishment of the camp was that the girls began to realise that the power to change their world lies with them!

Over the period, after every camp, the participants are asked for feedback on the learning that the camp initiated and also the impact it had on them. Some of the responses are:

1. Encouragement to self-discipline;
2. Motivation to fulfil their dreams;
3. Self-assertion;
4. Use of their leisure time in a positive manner;
5. Generated interest in creativity;
6. Changes in behaviour and thinking;
7. Started thinking in practical and realistic manner;
8. Camps provided innovative and useful information in an interesting way;

9. Made them aware about hygiene and sanitation;
10. Made them aware about their physical and nutritional status; and
11. Made emotional bonding with other participants and inculcated teamwork.

The programme was reviewed by an external resource person Savitri Subramaniam[1] in 2014. She endorsed the framework of the camp and made several useful suggestions. Many of these were incorporated in subsequent camps.

Over the past 18 years, nearly 1,000 girls have participated in these camps and have become better informed, more articulate, and more confident. Hopefully, many of them have become 'change agents' in their own way.

Note

1. Evaluation Report and Recommendations: Adolescent Girls Camp, by Savitri Subramanian (June, 2014).

10

Nurturing Lifelong Active Citizens

A 5th Space Approach

Malavika Pavamani, Neha Buch,
and Ishanee Bhattacharyya

Introduction

India is home to 243 million adolescents—20 per cent of the world's adolescents. One in every 5th person in India is an adolescent (Census of India, 2011). This demographic bulge offers India a rare opportunity to reap the dividend of being a relatively young nation. This opportunity will fully bear fruit only when the young people are able to realise their potential as active citizens and self-aware, deeply empathetic, inclusive, system thinking, and socially responsible leaders who will be able to create positive social change for themselves and the larger society today and in the future.

> Citizenship is that, which makes us participative, proactive and responsible towards society. The core values of citizenship include democracy, social justice, equality, peace, respect. Active citizenship refers to the ability of (young) people to be engaged in social action in every walk of life. Where people

> take ownership for common spaces and act to make change by addressing important social justice issues. This citizenship is boundary less ... not defined by state, caste, religion, language ... .
>
> *Excerpt from a presentation by Meenu Venkateswaran, CEO, Pravah (2005–10) at Nurturing Active Citizenship among Youth in India: A Consultation*

Active citizenship involves a journey from blaming to claiming ownership for addressing and finding solutions to concerns, conflicts, and issues in our lives. The kernel lies in being able to build our capacities to be able to see the fine threads that connect us and make us interdependent. It is this ability to see and feel the connection—the 'to' in what we at Pravah call the 'self to society' journey, which can make all the difference in 'one act' of active citizenship by a young person to becoming a 'lifelong' boundaryless active citizen.

While the definition of adolescent can differ from culture to culture, it is generally accepted that the time referred to as adolescence is the period between childhood and adulthood, a sort of 'no man's land' or a preparatory phase.

The dominant theories of adolescence do not acknowledge adolescents as capable and contributing members of society, even though adolescents in India contribute a significant part of the family income, and especially in the case of girls, also take on a fair amount of domestic responsibilities. In fact, in most cases, there is no space for adolescents in the decision-making or to express openly—whether it is in the family, in school, or in the community. Their opinions are not solicited. Instead, their parents or guardians are custodians of their wards' real needs and represent their best interests.

At the same time, the time old adage of 'now you have grown up' is often heard by adolescents from the 'adults' along with the said and unsaid expectations that go along. Unfortunately, responsibility and ownership both have to be taken on and experienced. They cannot be given. Similarly, wisdom or the capacity for insight and judgment, and therefore informed and responsible decision-making, can only come through experience.

Therein lies the gap. So how does an adolescent become an active citizen without any concrete opportunity to learn and experience the connection with the context outside of their own with 'others' across the boundaries of caste, class, gender, religion, and ideologies? How can an adolescent take informed decisions without first understanding how the mind is made up and how to take a decision. Without having access to a safe space where s/he is able to practice decision taking and making, how can an adolescent learn how to take responsibility and ownership without having an opportunity to lead and be mentored through that process and supported in learning from both the successes and the mistakes? And how can an adult or a young person do any of these effectively without experiencing them in their adolescence?

> Imagine that I have a pair of size 10 shoes. I gift them to you. Will you take them? ... . No right? Because your shoe size maybe different, you may want sandals not shoes, or you may take them and give them away to someone else ... the gift will be of no use to you. For young people as well, too many size 10 shoes do not work. It is therefore critical that the designs for the adolescent programmes are made by including them understanding their issues and making them a part of the design process.
> *A young person at The International Association for Adolescent Health, 11th World Congress on Adolescent Health.*

What is needed is an 'Adolescent Development' approach where the emphasis is as much on the transformation of the young person as is on the transformation of the world through the young person. This approach involves processes that are adolescent centred and focus on developing their leadership potential. It places the young person as a partner in addressing development problems while nurturing their potential as change agents. Thus, it strengthens the connection between the self and society. This we believe is imperative for there to be sustainable change with young people becoming lifelong active citizens.

The starting point will therefore need to be building our understanding of the ocean that resides in the drop, that is, a young person, and then designing an appropriate intervention.

How can Adolescents be Empowered to Become Active Citizens?

The answer lies in creating safe empowering and enabling spaces, or what Pravah calls the 5th Space.

What is a 5th Space?

Typically a young person spends time at home with family, hanging out with friends, in leisure, or at college/workplace. Traditionally these four spaces make up their universe. In all these spaces, their worldview derives from an already given legacy through a lens which society has donned for millennia. Beyond this received wisdom in his/her time, don't they need another space that allows them to create their own understanding of the world?

1. To understand themselves, develop, and grow;
2. To look at social issues from a systemic lens and see how they are connected to them;
3. To deal with conflicts within and around them in society; and
4. To take action that benefits them and the surroundings.

This is the 5th space. It is a space where young people develop a psycho-social worldview, which answers the question 'Who are we?' (we as in humans—a social species) as opposed to 'Who am I?' This view allows young people to understand and define their connection to the world as it is. The 5th space makes the relationships in the other four spaces count by nourishing and enriching the capacities of young people to take effective and responsible action. The 5th space believes that self-transformation is the first step towards creating change in our relationships and in society.

Figure 1

The 5th Space

To get the young people involved, the interventions must be co-created with young people and architect spaces for experiencing the real world without preaching. It must offer tools and processes that enable young people to understand how their minds are made up and be able to choose how they would like for them to be made up. It must enable them to cut through the fluff and the stories about their own selves and about the world in order to interpret reality. Only then will they be able to withstand the overwhelming push to 'conform'.

Peer dialogues, group actions, creative methodologies, and a space to experiment and lead are all critical for young people—creating a strong 'pull'. Facilitators need to hold these spaces such that it is felt to be safe and non-judgemental. In a world that is so polarised, it is important to ensure that the interventions bring together heterogeneous groups of young people to journey together. It is only then that true relationships can be fostered and dangerous singular stories can be broken, and a new more informed worldview can be created.

The 5th space approach creates designs that take the young people from Me to We journeys. The individual is encouraged to grow into their personal roles and from here, the natural extension into a responsible citizen is emphasised where the focus is on taking informed stances and action in life. No right way is emphasised but skills and processes of arriving at one's own stances are elaborated. Principles of going beyond stereotypes, appreciating diversity, and practicing tolerance are internalised through experiential learning processes.

Active Citizenship at SCOUL (Scale with Soul): Praya Sapna to Sapna Apna

The Context

The Ministry of Youth and Sports Affairs (Government of India) and UNFPA have been collaborating since 2004 on addressing the health and development needs of out-of-school adolescents. Between 2008 and 2012, Nehru Yuva Kendra Sangathan (NYKS) implemented the Adolescent Health and Development project.

With the support of UNFPA, they established 3,840 teen clubs across 64 districts. In 2013, a field review showed the challenges in attracting and retaining out to out-of-school adolescents. The number of teen clubs was now reduced to 1,860 across 62 blocks in 10 districts across the five states of Bihar, Madhya Pradesh, Maharashtra, Rajasthan, and Odisha.

In 2014, Pravah was invited to support the re-conceptualisation of the Teen Club programme, develop the curriculum, build capacities of the project staff, and mentor, review, and support the state-level Non-Governmental Organizations (NGOs) and the NYKS project team through the implementation process.

What We Did

Our first response was to start the process of reimagining the vision and curriculum. Based on our conversations with adolescents, peer educators, and the different partners who had been engaged in the past, we co-created the new vision of the programme: 'To create empowering spaces that nurtures and inspires adolescents to identify and fulfil their aspirations for a happy and healthy life'

Till now, the focus had been on how to create an effective adolescent health programme. This unfortunately was a little like the size 10 shoe. It was not really something that the out-of-school adolescents were really interested in. We therefore decided to focus on 'Sapna' or 'Dream' and the 'Prayas' or 'Effort' that would be needed to realise them in order for them to have happy and healthy lives.

The Psycho-Social Approach

The key to this was to construct a mode around the framework of dreams that was simple, iterative, and engaging, one that could be opened enough for contextualisation. There had to be consistency in the quality of the experience across the teen clubs as well as belief and capacities built in the larger system around self to society journeys. We were able to do the above by ensuring the intervention designed had the 5th space principles as the core.

Guiding principles for the re-strategised teen club programme:

1. *Journey-based instead of event-based*: The curriculum was designed as a leadership learning journey that takes the participants from what they know to what they do not know. Delivered in a modular form such that each segment is complete within itself and easy to absorb and yet strung together as a progression. Mentoring processes support the holding together of the journey.
2. *Self to society*: To ensure that participants were able to take ownership of the larger society, it was essential that they were able to locate themselves in the larger picture and see the self in an interdependent relationship with the world. The curriculum was designed to connect personal aspirations and passion with larger issues facing the community around them.
3. *Builds critical thinking*: The ability to arrive at answers by developing the skill of asking questions, seeking facts, and interpreting the multiple viewing points was one of the key principles guiding the curriculum design. It therefore did not focus on giving answers but instead on how to develop the faculties of critical thinking and enable participants to become self-directed learners.
4. *Informed self- and issue-based reflection*: The process of learning was complete only when there was both reflection and action. The curriculum was designed to ensure that there is a combination of both theory and reflection spaces as well as action spaces.
5. *Close to the reality and culture of participants*: The curriculum had a real-world connection and had contextual examples created keeping in mind the reality and the context of participants.
6. *Learner led and learner owned*: The learning process was in the hands of the learner and they were made in charge.

7. *Problem solving and application-based learning*: To ensure that the participants learn flexible knowledge, effective problem-solving skills, self-directed learning, effective collaboration skills, and intrinsic motivation, they would engage with open-ended problems to experience solving them. This active, contextual, non-linear, and transformative learning is imperative in today's dynamic world. This experiential learning method allowed for the learners to play an active role and create avenues for experimentation.
8. *Fun and interesting*: It is essential to create hope and not a sense of cynicism through the journey. Understanding young people and using creative methodologies to ensure that even as we go about this serious business we approach and treat it with a sense of lightness.
9. *Creates a safe and empowering space*: Self-disclosure and creating change requires a conducive and sound environment for the learner. The curriculum strived to create a space where learners could fully express without the fear of being uncomfortable, unwelcome, or unsafe.
10. *Forward dynamic built in*: Design flow was based on a psychosocial approach such that it creates an internal motivation to move forward, rather than an external push from the facilitator.

Curriculum Framework

The adolescents through the course of this journey identified multiple dreams—dream of a comfortable standard of living, dream of good relationships, dream of status and respect, dream of a good health, dream of a healthy village, and dream of leading change.

Dreams however are not enough. It is critical to identify the effort that needs to go into realising those dreams.

Since we were running this across 1,860 teen clubs, it was critical that the framework of the curriculum allowed for easy

Figure 2

The Praya Sapna Curriculum Framework

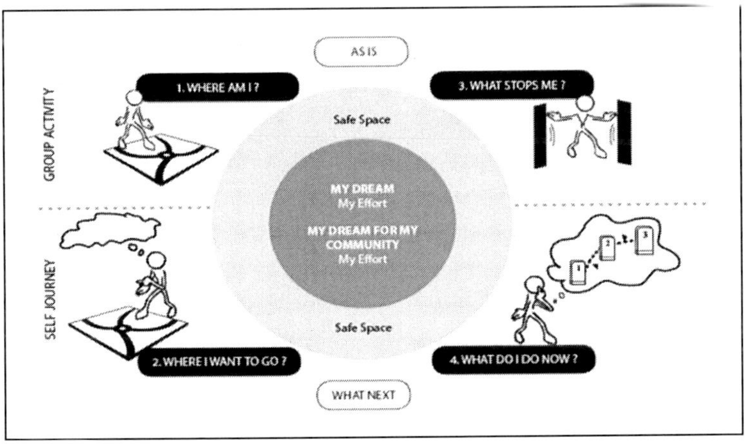

customisation and contextualisation and was simple enough to be understood.

The four-step framework as shown in Figure 2 was able to fulfil both the needs. It was simple and could be easily contextualised, allowing for relatability owing to its emergent nature and enabling us to ensure scale with soul or 'Scoul'.

The Cascade Model and the Role of the Facilitator

Being a programme at scale, Pravah was not working with adolescents directly. We were responsible for working with the district programme officers and other state NGO and official personnel, who in turn cascade the training to the adolescent peer volunteers who then would work with the adolescents.

Typically, programmes focus on technical and content-based training of facilitators. However, interventions that are trying to empower young people and create safe spaces for that purpose need facilitators who have experienced an empowering and enabling space and buy into the need for it. Facilitators who may never have experienced democratic, safe, and empowering spaces cannot be expected to create them for young people. Technical and content-based inputs can be understood and passed on through trainings, but the soft skill part and how to set up and hold 5th spaces require experiential learning and capacity building.

Besides building the capacities of the facilitators to identify elements and culture of the 5th space and to build them in their own contexts, the curriculum cascade was supported through a journey of mentoring and handholding by the Pravah facilitators. The curriculum was tested at the level of the Ashram Paryavaran Vidyalaya (APV) being able to transact it effectively with the adolescents in their community, and not just at the Pravah facilitators transacting it with the other facilitators. This pushed us to keep simplifying the curriculum till it worked effectively all across.

Journey at a Glance

This intervention was designed as a journey, taking into account the different stakeholders of the system that it was situated in. To embed the self to society journeys with the 5th space principles, it was critical for capacities to be built at every level from the adolescents to Physical Educations (PEs) and block to district staff. The design kept the motivation, energy, and needs of different stakeholders in mind such that they also built their conviction around the programme by experiencing a learning journey for themselves.

There was an ownership building workshop to create a buy in for the programme amongst all the functionaries. This was followed by a drive to mobilise and select peer educators who were adolescents from the community having the passion and will as well as some experience to take on the role.

The staff (district project officer, district technical facilitator, adolescent peer volunteer, and block technical facilitator) went through multiple enablement workshops, which laid emphasis on their own capacities to mentor the peer educators and support their learning journeys. Since it ran as a training of trainers' model, the functionaries experienced all the sessions as participants first to build empathy for their audience and understand the nuances of the content. Being part of the 5th space themselves, which was safe, authentic, fun-filled, co-created, and invested in their learning enabled them to create such spaces in the peer training workshops that they further facilitated.

The re-formulated peer leader led teen clubs came into being and had meetings on a fortnightly basis. The peer educator trainings run by the staff not only prepared them for the content to be transacted but built their capacities to create an empowering learner-led and centric space within the teen club that established a strong pull for the adolescents to be a part of the meetings regularly. The staff invested in the self to motivate peer educators in a way that built their confidence as leaders who could further influence adolescents to build positive change for themselves and within the larger community through social action.

The staff started viewing this engagement beyond one-time training with the PEs. They started taking ownership for the leadership experience of the PEs and the journeys of the adolescents in the teen clubs. Therefore, the journey included field visits to understand the challenges faced by the PEs and support in co-facilitating identified of the sessions. There was handholding and mentoring of the PEs, which led to the monitoring being collaborative and solution driven rather than questioning and blame.

The curriculum had community action projects as a critical component to encourage learning through real-world application. The young people engaged with the community to collectively identify issues recognised their own strengths as a team and created a robust action plan. There were roles given to the teen club members as well as the community, government departments, and local organisations. The teams executed the plans on action days, which were followed by reflection spaces to capture the learning.

There was a space created for the staff and the programme team to come together in monthly governance reviews, express

Figure 3

Journey Design with Milestones

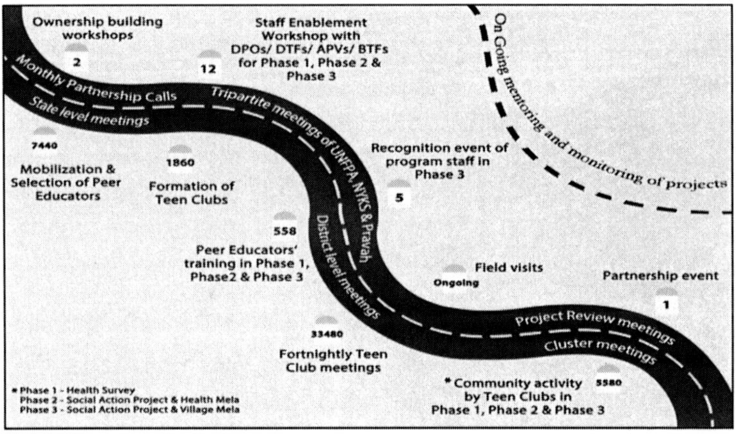

their ongoing concerns, collaborate on solutions, share their learning, and create corrective course of action. This brought in a culture of reflection and action in the team and created a safe space for authentic sharing where the team felt that they were on the same page and there was no blame.

Impact of the Programme

The programme impact was done through self-reporting done by the peer educators. The indicators mapped were across internal change as well as external action. There were qualitative stories of change collected from the teen club members, peer educators, block- and district-level staff, as well as members from the community, including the voice of the peer educators and co-creating the evaluation keeping their reporting at the centre.

> Field staff across all five states report that teen clubs have given a space for adolescents to share their feelings—the session on status and respect has brought out some stories of feeling disrespected (due to case, class, gender discrimination, etc.) that had never been told to anyone and converted that experience into something constructive for them.

Figure 4

Impact of the Teen Club Programme

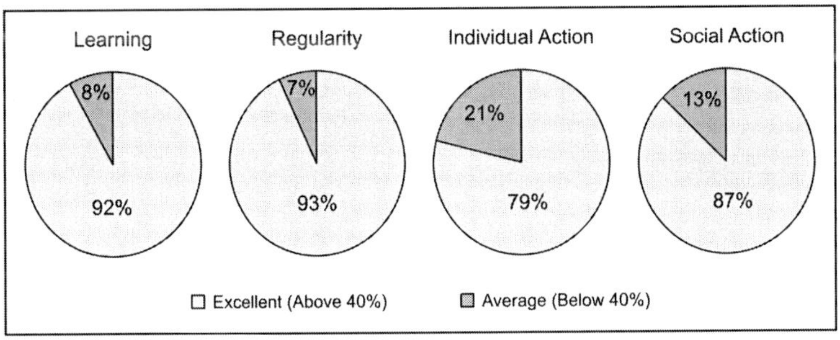

- ✓ Learning has been enhanced due to simplicity and relevance of Praya Sapna curriculum.
- ✓ Regularity and attendance of the meetings has been enhanced due to adolescents having sense of ownership for the space.
- ✓ The curriculum inspires adolescents to have realisation of their dreams and make efforts to achieve their individual dreams.
- ✓ Teen Club members are coming together for the 'Social Action Project' examples – 'Malaria Eradication Drive, Stopping Alcoholism etc.

Note: This analysis is done on the basis of self reported data by Peer Educators as per their field level programme understanding and experience post Phase 2. Probability of subjectivity in the data, must be considered*.

> The District Technical Facilitator (DTF) of Gaya rightly described cluster meeting as the 'life line' of the programme. The cluster meetings have created a sense of bonding and network of PEs in many clusters. Many PEs have started supporting meetings of other teen clubs near their villages. Purnea and Gaya teams conduct these meetings in the 10 villages in rotation—this has helped immensely in building community support for the programme.

Another major achievement is the number of out-of-school adolescents we have been able to reach out to this time due to constant focus on the group. Bihar, Madhya Pradesh, Rajasthan, and Odisha have many out-of-school adolescents coming to meetings regularly like never before. The idea of having out-of-school PEs and getting PEs to conduct adolescent survey have played a significant role in this endeavour.

Praya Sapna to Sapna Apna

With the closure of teen club programme in June 2016, a total of 7,440 trained PEs became available as an important resource in the field; it was proposed that UNFPA establish a funding scheme aimed at channelling grants to select vibrant and trained PEs. This programme was built on the lessons learned from the 2.5 years of teen club Praya Sapna journey to deepen their current journey.

PEs were central to the project. They were the final link in the cascade. The selection of the PEs took place with support from the community, which not only gave credence to their role but also helped to keep the project rooted to the community. Community involvement throughout was useful for the success of the project.

Deepening of the learnings and insights of Praya Sapna journeys of teen club programme helped in effective implementation of community action projects.

Insights gained and capacities learnt during this journey were carried forward to the next level of the programme, which helped the PEs to realise their dreams of addressing larger community issues and to work as a collective through the project that was identified by them. They got a period of 2–3 months to work on their dream and were supported by the challenge fund under 'Praya Sapna Sapna Apna' programme.

These developed 'Community Action Projects' were the means of replicating the learning's of teen club Praya Sapna journey and aimed to deepen the elements of self, relationship, and community inclusion within the project.

Community action projects followed the following guidelines:

1. Duration of 2–3 months;
2. It needed to have the advocacy component, be participatory, have social and entrepreneurial approach, and be non-confrontational in nature;
3. There was no inclusion of the direct element of infrastructure development; and
4. Proposed ideas were built with consensus of the team/cluster and yet could have individual community or club-level aspects focussed within the action project.

Figure 5

Action Projects Across States

200 rallies	150 nukkad nataks	250 community meetings
40 health melas	1,500 toilets made functional	16 government departments engaged with

The journey from Praya Sapna to Sapna Apna has been critical in demonstrating that when we are able to ensure that we empathise with young people, bring them on as co-creators, and engage with the entire ocean that resides in the drop that is that young person, then not only will they transform their own selves, they will also transform the world in the present as well as in the future through active citizenship.

The important thing is to remember to figure out what the adolescents really want rather than pushing the size 10 shoes that we may have in our backpack.

Active citizenship involves bridging the gap between the self and the society, and transforming the relationship between the self and community. This involves a transformation from me to we through a process of building self-awareness and inspiring young people to understand and engage with social issues so that they can initiate and lead citizenship action and bring about social change.

Principles of 5th space

1. It is their space!
    - To build ownership for this space and its vision, it needs to be co-created in partnership with young people.
2. It encourages trust in a fun, joyful, and transformatory way
    - The culture of the 5th space needs to attract young people by encouraging trust and openness and by creating opportunities for young people to take on leadership roles, so they can experiment without fear, make mistakes, and learn in the presence of experienced facilitators and supportive peers.

3 It initiates learning through experience

- In the 5th space, trained facilitators support young people to reflect and act. Action alone is not enough to learn about the self and the world. Reflection before and after the process is essential for effective learning.

4. It facilitates self-exploration
    - The 5th space should take young people through an understanding from what they know to what they do not—exploring to understand themselves better by reflecting on the following questions:
        - How deeply do they relate to others?
        - To what extent is their journey influenced by their destination?
        - How well do they know themselves?
        - How well equipped are they to undertake their journey?
        - How well informed is their worldview?
5. It foregrounds the NOW, not the future
    - Instead of focussing on the future and preparing young people to become tomorrow's leaders, the 5th space creates opportunities for young people to act today in the here and now.
6. Entrepreneurship promotion
    - The 5th space must aim to meet the aspirations of young people and also meet the socio-economic needs and hence should create opportunities to connect them to sustainable market models and processes.
7. It is a hangout zone beyond borders
    - The 5th space provides young people with opportunities to connect with peers from diverse background so that they can understand different perspectives, develop their own opinions, and build skills to engage with issues they feel deeply about.
8. It organically renews the space back in their own lives.
    - The 5th space spawns more of its kinds by inspiring others to adopt these principles back in the other four spaces. It becomes a self-facilitated space where they

constantly let the world consciously transform them as a person.

9. It is a sensitive space

    - The 5th space is sensitive to their feelings and not just the volunteering work they do. It hence deals with the whole young person where feelings, relationships, and opinions —nothing is side-lined.

11

Understanding the Constitution

Agrini's Work with Adolescents

Navendu Mishra and Gourav Jaiswal

Introduction

Agrini Samaj Kalyan Samiti is working in Seoni district of Madhya Pradesh since 2009 in the field of education. In the past eight years, there have been many programmes and innovative interventions that Agrini has undertaken—quality preschool education in anganwadis and Shikshalaya knowledge resource centre are few major ones. Agrini also runs a community school, which promises to slowly become a model in itself. This paper briefly describes Agrini's work on increasing the understanding of the constitution among adolescents.

Constitutional Literacy in Adolescents' Lives

Shikshalaya

Agrini's work to increase constitutional literacy at individual and institutional levels is now five years old. During these years, Agrini's Shikshalaya, a knowledge resource centre, facilitates coming together and exchange of knowledge amongst rural youth. It also provided a much needed platform to disseminate know how on local self-government as much as it promoted active participation at panchayat and gram sabha level.

Out of 1,000 youngsters, only 10 per cent understand the basic structure of panchayat. Only 5 per cent understand about duties of sarpanch, sachiv, panch, and other panchayat representatives and executives. Other than this, only 2 per cent understood about three-level panchayati raj arrangement and roles of jila panchayat and janpad panchayat in the structure. It needs to be emphasised that because only 2 per cent had an understanding about the members of the legislative assembly and parliament. Being in the age group of 15–18 years, soon the youth would be a first-time voter in 2–3 years. It is pertinent to ponder, given their limited understanding of the democratic system, on what basis would the young choose their representatives?

The Shikshalaya acted as a place where youngsters were engaged in activities and sessions on central, state, and local governance and also about different government schemes that they can avail of. It might be mentioned that Mahatma Gandhi Rural Employment Guarantee Act (MNREGA) in its initial stages, when discussed at length, prompted the youth to become not only more active and aware as citizens but also more confident in their personal lives.

The impact of constitutional awareness in youth can be seen through the following incident. Shikshalaya—an independent co-learning space for rural youth was set up by Agrini in the tribal block of Kurai in Seoni district. During a session on MNREGA in Shikshalaya, the youth much to their surprise learnt that MNREGA payment and work data can be easily accessed via the internet on the MNREGA management information system (MIS). Putting their computer literacy to use, the youngsters then decided to check the MIS and, at the first glimpse itself, found several discrepancies in the payment records for Kurai gram panchayat. The most glaring inconsistency was the false labour records.

This was informed to the village elders, women, labourers, and farmers. A protest against these corrupt practices was then planned at the village level with a sole agenda to ensure the implementation of social audit. This protest grew and attracted considerable media attention. This caused the central government's Rural Development Department to intervene in the matter, and an order was passed to conduct social audit in 62 panchayats in Kurai block. Thus, social audit was successfully conducted in 62 gram panchayats and a public hearing was also held. About 1 lakh MNREGA workers were benefitted as a result.

Understanding Constitutional Values and Development with Adolescents Using the Principles of 5th Space

As constitutional values, namely justice, liberty, equality, and fraternity, play an important role in personal and societal development in our lives, so do the values of the 5th space freedom, which helps us in understanding youngsters and working with them. Principles of 5th space when practiced on ground energise the youth.

Age old system in our society leaves little or no personal space to adolescents. To add insult to injury, generally speaking, they are considered as incapable of taking their own decisions. 5th space principles furnish that space where they can take their own decisions without fear of being judged or of emotional subjugation. This then helps them gain the confidence they need for self-development.

UnManifesto Campaign

Agrini conducted UnManifesto campaign from October 2013 to March 2014 in partnership with Community Youth Collective. During this campaign, Agrini reached out to almost 2,000 adolescents from three vidhan sabha areas of Seoni district, namely Seoni, Barghat, and Keolari. Twenty schools were targeted to reach out to 2,000 youngsters. Our agenda was primarily to reach out to these youngsters, understand their issues, and help them be heard by the political parties and civil society leaders so that their manifesto's in 2014 lok sabha elections may to some extent reflect the youth issues.

One of the major issues during this campaign was to reach out to adolescents and introduce them to a democratic system and to the concept of active citizenship. Initially, when we questioned the youth whether they are citizens—18 per cent of them said 'No'. Shocking as the answer was, we delved deeper with exhausting conversations. The prevalent belief in the youth was that only those eligible to vote are citizens, and citizen's rights are exclusive to those who do! Also, in case of fundamental rights, their belief was that they hold good only for adults. After our conversations and sessions, we were able to dispel these misgivings about the idea of citizenship. We also discussed that once a foetus becomes 3 months old, our constitution considers it as an individual entity. And thus, rights are not limited to the idea of voting alone. We also discussed about their rights as citizens and how a citizen is not only a voter but has also becomes eligible to contest municipal or panchayat elections after the age of 21 years and can contest other elections for constitutional positions after the age of 25 years. According to the constitution, the system is applicable to every citizen, and it is the constitutional duty of every citizen to abide by it. After these orientation sessions, they were confident about raising their voice and keenly aware of the importance of understanding the constitutional rights and duties. In due course, our outreach programme had touched more than 10,000 adolescents. During this campaign, not only basic demands such as electricity, roads, and water but also national issues such as women safety, education, health, and employment came to be centre stage. Other than this, the campaign helped generate an interest in the local panchayat elections to be conducted in 2015. The initial extreme indifference now had given way to raising questions on the working of panchayat, stake of citizens, and accountability of public representatives. They were now more interested in issues raised by national parties, stories in newspapers, and local or neighbourhood-centric issues.

This campaign is a conclusive proof that our system fails to provide a citizen-friendly atmosphere in general and an adolescent-sensitive one in particular. To make matters worse, the education system does not ignite young minds. Socially, a family is the first incubator of duties and rights for a child, and it in no uncertain terms breeds in the young apathy as a citizen!

Constitutional Values and Agrini Public School

After working for 4 years on ground, in November 2013, we realised that we need our own space to disseminate our ideas and ideals. As a result, we conceptualised the idea of Agrini Public School, which was not only a school and a resource centre but also an innovation space. From its very inception, the set of values to be inculcated was our overwhelming concern. And to address it, we needed to examine in great detail basic questions such as 'What is the purpose of education?', 'Who is an ideal citizen?', 'What is an ideal society?', and 'How is our institution going to be an important link in finding answers to these very pertinent questions?'. One probable answer was to build an institution based on human values. But we needed a point of reference to fall back upon. What better than the constitution of India that clearly states liberty, justice, fraternity, and equality as core values as our surviving manual. Also, its democratic, secular, and socialist ideals gave us the required bed rock to build our institution on! Aware that our education system did not incorporate these ideals as much as was needed to produce committed citizens, our next step was to lay foundations of an institution that would fill the above glaring gap.

Community Participation

We at Agrini have always believed in community participation since our inception. To ensure this participation in the newly found institution, we initiated a dialogue with community from its very inception. Depending on its history, every community has its own perception about education and it is difficult to convince them to try an innovative idea without engaging them in a dialogue about it. This being an educational intervention, all the activities were going to happen within the community, and this made community participation extremely crucial.

Parents as Stakeholders

Manifesto is a very important tool of democratic process. During a discussion on elections in Agrini run Shikshalaya, young students expressed how votes were won with liquor and money during local gram panchayat elections. And in the process, the main agenda of villagers is lost. To avoid this, election manifesto could act as a useful tool.

Shikshalaya members, local youngsters, with the help of Agrini visited different villages in the area to spread awareness about the importance of manifesto among citizens. This act led to the creation of election manifestos by village sarpanch and panch candidates across 27 different gram panchayat during elections. Issues such as the need for proper infrastructure, roads, toilets, housing, drinking water, etc were identified and candidates made to support the same! Because parents are an integral part of the community, we decided to give parents a bigger space in decisions-making in the school. Parents were going to play a very important role in this, for example, if we want to propagate 'Liberty' as a value in school, it was important that the parents adhere to it at home also. In view of the fact that adolescents spend a lot of time at home and in society, the need to build a transparent bond between parents, their wards, and the school was felt. Hence, a school parent's committee was formed, which not only took financial, managerial decisions for the school but also guided school management on other issues.

Participation of Teachers

Teachers play a very important role in adolescents' lives, as most of the adolescents try to imitate their teachers and follow them beyond logic. In this case, it becomes extremely important for teachers to live the values that we were envisioning for our students to imbibe. Thus, we started involving teachers in every decision-making, may it be social, financial, or any other issue of student welfare. This ensured an important space for teachers in policy decisions and future planning of the institution.

Participation of Adolescents

The biggest challenge was to create space for adolescents where they can actually experience values such as liberty, equality, fraternity, and justice. To create this space, tenants from 5th space played an important role. Value education can only be experiential, and to make it happen, we had to design those experiences that can take students in that journey where they can practice them. To ensure this journey, we decided to involve values such as non-violence, liberty, love, and justice, and to practice the precept—equality, cooperation, growth, change, etc. was included in our curriculum. To ensure everyone's participation, some procedures were made mandatory.

1. First was a regular dialogue between parents, student's parliament, teachers, and school management through monthly meetings to counter current challenges and future planning. These meetings were platforms to discuss resource management to achieve the planned goals. It also acts as a common information platform for everyone to come together and stay updated on every crucial issue.

   The above was held on the second Saturday of every month.

2. Workshops with parents on different issues related to adolescents are routinely held. Purpose of these workshops is to introduce parents to current challenges of adolescence. Parents generally are aware of these challenges, but social stereotypes prevent them from focussing on them.

3. To take the institute towards financial self-sustainability, a parent's committee was formed and entrusted the task of taking financial decisions of fee waiver for students from financially weaker class. We try to ensure representation of all sections of society in the committee.

4. Formation of a student's cabinet is also a part of Right to Education Act, but we at Agrini are trying to take it to another level with our student's parliament. This

parliament not only meets weekly to takes decisions for day-to-day management of school, but also meets monthly with teachers and parents to be a part of a major future plan and policy decisions.

In our experience, in all these years, we have learned that if we wish to take value-based education to adolescents, we will have to involve the community and make the complete process inclusive to generate a sense of ownership within all stakeholders.

Constitutional Understanding in Adolescents through Schools

After working for all these years on constitutional values with students, we started realising change in ourselves, but still there was a long way to go. Along with 'We the People' (another organisation working on constitutional education), we started working to understand constitution and constitutional structure, which later resulted in building our own understanding of constitutional structure. This experience gave us a clear understanding of administrative structure, political system, and local governance. This highlighted the need of involving constitutional studies in education.

Although it is already in curriculum, we realised the need of more emphasis on this. Then we started working with schools and designed workshops for students based on constitutional topics in their curriculum. In the past 2 years, we have reached out to more than 300 adolescents by this means. On the basis of this experience, now we are working to develop our understanding on using idea of 'experiential learning' for this purpose. While working on constitutional values with youngsters, one comes across a lot of interesting experiences. One such incident happened when we came across a chapter on *Birsa Munda* in the class VIII NCERT (National Council of Educational Research and Training) text book of History. There is clear distinction in the way and tone of *Birsa Munda*'s narration as compared with other historical leaders. It seems to be less respectful. For example, the Mughal Emperor Aurangzeb is described as 'the last most powerful Emperor in the Mughal empire', whereas Birsa Munda is said to be 'a tribal who was observed to walk around'. This was noticed by the students, and they decided to take up this discussion in the student parliament. During the student parliament's session, it was agreed upon by both tribal and non-tribal members of the student parliament that a letter should be sent to NCERT, drawing attention to the insensitivity of this narration and a correction in the text should be requested. This incident shows that when constitutional values are included in experiential learning of students, they tend to grow as responsible citizens. School faculty, administrations, or even parents need to give subjects of social science the importance they deserve. More often than not, social sciences as against Maths, Science, and English are considered less important. Some teachers are of the opinion that these subjects are so easy that students can study themselves. Yet, in a democracy, it is very clear that subjects of such importance enhance understanding of citizenship and impart a cohesiveness in society and it is wrong to dismiss them as an unnecessary part of curriculum. After being a part of this programme, more than 40 per cent students started taking interest in discussions about the constitution.

During this programme, we did experiential workshops on preamble of constitution, fundamental rights, fundamental duties, constitutional bodies, structure of state, etc. Also, we tried to create a thought connect within students on how fundamental rights are connected to decisions by courts, laws and acts, decisions by governments, and government schemes.

Samvidhan Live—The Jagrik Project

Samvidhan Live refers to living our constitution. The country celebrates Republic day on 26th January every year as a national festival since 1950. Yet, when we questioned 3,000 people 'weather they have seen their constitution', they answered a 'No' and did not in any way relate to it.

All these were people from different occupations but are still playing an important role in different positions in our constitutional structure. It was really surprising that even after

67 years of our constitution, it remained shrouded in mystery for the larger part of our citizenry. And we realised that if adults display such apathy and lack constitutional understanding, little wonder then for the adolescents—the future of our nation—it is at best a legal document and at worst something that their forefathers drafted. And can our goal of laying a foundation of strong citizenship ever be realised without the basic understanding of the constitution by the adolescents? Through Samvidhan Live, we reached out to more than 400 students and tried to gauge their level of understanding about the constitution. We rolled out the session with a perennial question to the students: 'Weather they had seen a copy of the constitution or had ever read any part of it?' No brownie points for guessing the answer—majorly a 'No'! It was really surprising because the preamble of Indian constitution, fundamental rights, fundamental duties, etc. are printed in almost all subject textbooks that are subscribed for the students. That we kickstarted in schools our campaign to spread knowledge about our constitution was in view of the above prevalent dismal state of affairs!

Through this campaign, we reached out to youngsters in schools and colleges via workshops with an objective of creating awareness about our constitution and constitutional values. In general perception, the constitution is considered as a rule book, which is useful either for administrative officers or politicians, and it has nothing to do with general citizens. At our first stage of campaign, we started working with youngsters and observed results when youngsters started connecting fundamental rights and duties in their daily life. The outcome was extremely encouraging for us as we could see the drastic changes in the understanding and behaviour of youngsters. Effect on their social, political, and personal life was clearly visible. This was also helping them develop a better and deeper understanding on national issues such as unemployment, reservations, and education. Also, understanding of fundamental duties was helping them be active and responsible citizens.

Four youngsters of Seoni, Satish, Arpit, Anand and Vibhor, have been the most proactive during Samvidhan Live. They took up the issue of cleaning Seoni's iconic Dal Sagar Lake as a part of Samvidhan Live. During its campaign, it dawned upon them that as citizens, it is our fundamental duty to protect and conserve our natural resources. They connected with the city administration and other citizens in the city personally and over social media. Although this did not in any way impact the society in a big way, their effort created a dialogue about the issue that mattered to the public—so in essence, a journey of a thousand miles had begun with one small step! Four months later, in May 2017, few local citizens along with city administration bodies began the work of cleaning the lake. All four youngsters that were part of the Operation Clean Lake not only volunteered but also supervised and contributed to the work in progress. Satish would supervise the work every night after closing his shop. Anand, Vibhor, and Arpit took stock of the progress regularly and shared these updates with locals. Surely this was possible because of one simple act of underlying the importance of being an active citizen! Constitutional values create a sense of ownership within citizens. As a citizen, these values help us to connect with our natural resources in a more responsible and organic way.

12

Nurturing Social Change

Case Study of Rubaroo in Hyderabad

Monisha Vemavarapu, Hema Khatri, Neha Swain, Shubhi Dwivedi, and Balendu Rashmi

About Rubaroo

Rubaroo simply means 'coming face-to-face' with myself, society, and issues around me, my choices, my values, my fears, and everything that becomes my identity. For the founding team at Rubaroo, it was a word that encompassed what all of us believed in when we came to found the organisation. It linked our life journeys to the turning points of finding our passion—a space, which nurtured our potential to challenge and breakaway from the conditioning of society. Also, a space that gave us the freedom to choose consciously, question, and learn to be change makers. Taking from its meaning, Rubaroo aims to be an organisation where adolescents and young people can come together to learn from each other. It aims to be an empowering space where young people co-create the space to understand themselves better, understand issues and take action in society, and nourish relationships to become socially conscious leaders in their own capacity.

Rubaroo's Vision: To create an inclusive, just, and equitable world where individuals transcend boundaries through an engagement—both with the self and society.

Rubaroo Mission: To create a platform—safe and inclusive for young people to access opportunities of learning and self-development.

Objective: Building leadership for social change through a psychosocial approach.

How we aim to do this:

1. Facilitate experiential learning journeys through exposure visits and camps;
2. Creating a physical space based on the principles and values of 5th space and offer activities, sessions, and projects to provide the relevant experience for volunteers;
3. Holding fortnightly sessions or activities to create self-awareness or/and through social issues;
4. With issue-based workshops and clubs. Mentoring self-development;
5. Offering skill/interest-based experimentation for young people to explore their passion; and
6. Partnering with organisations, NGOs, and institutes to create visibility while simultaneously working with the young.

Based in Hyderabad, Rubaroo aims to build spaces where school- and college-going young adults are nudged to explore and link their academic learning with realities around them. To make education and not just schooling, truly democratic and meaningful for every child or for that matter for any adult as well as for the parents and teachers, surely, both of these need to go hand in hand. Social spaces around us become critical in the growing-up phase of our adolescent life, as they often represent the age old handed-down values and beliefs from our family, friends, and other socialisation that has impacted us. We, at Rubaroo, believe that change begins by finding/co-creating spaces where individuals are enabled to challenge and question all that they have known or have been told by others about themselves and the world around them. It is important to do so because only by breaking down their own 'stories', and challenging themselves, they can unleash within them the potential to become conscious decision makers. Herman Hesse famously said in Siddhartha—'no one can walk your path for you'. We, at Rubaroo, invite young people to take a journey together, search for their path, to understand themselves just a little better, without all the masks and facades, diving deep into the scariest vulnerabilities and rising up with their strengths, through joy and sorrow, and then connecting back with what and who are around us.

Rubaroo began in the year 2013, and was informally called Pravah Pahal, then. In the first year, it was a platform to experiment with, understand, and gauge the perception of the work we aimed to do, with our partner institutes and participants. The response of the work that we did in the first year determined our way ahead both to the kind of work that was needed in Hyderabad and the kind of work that we wanted to do. Why adolescents? Adolescence and teenage years are formative years and critical in shaping a young person's choices, values, and decisions. In a country and culture such as ours, young people are often shrugged off, saying that they may not have the 'experience' or maturity in being able to understand what may be 'good' and what may be 'bad' for them. In such an age, we feel that it is extremely important to work with young people to be able to empower them, build an entrepreneurial spirit, foster decision-making and informed choices, stances, and be able to lead lives within their realm of choices.

Hence in the initial 3 years of Rubaroo, the focus was on working with adolescent girls and boys and within institutional frameworks where they may belong. Working with more than 3,000 adolescents on issues of interfaith, gender, early and child marriage, and in sustainable development, it has facilitated conversations on what it takes to nurture their potentials. We have also realised that along with working with adolescents, it becomes imperative to work with the ecosystem that supports and nurtures them. Our programmes aim to work with parents, community members, and teachers who impact a young person's life. In the schooling system, while there is a focus on academics,

Rubaroo also focusses on life skills and beyond to be able to create positive and active citizens by mentoring students to become leaders in their own capacity wherever they may be. We especially work with contextualising academic curriculums to influence young people to understand how their text book learning can be applied to real-world scenarios outside the classroom. It also creates a platform where they understand external issues from personal perspectives.

They are able to contextualise the issues of caste, gender, religion, nationalism, and other forms of identity-based discrimination. The young then no longer remain a third party! external (which they may often only come across in media). Infact, they internalise to see how it influences their relationships within their friends, family, and communities around them. Through the learning of 5th space, and as being part of the community The Youth Collective, Rubaroo has partnered with many campaigns where adolescents have the opportunity to engage with many of the above and identify what is that they want to change about themselves and in so doing permeate change in the people around them. The 5th space idea essentially allows them to focus on themselves and build a deeper understanding of themselves and to also enhance and nourish the relationships in the other four spaces around them of family, friends, education, and leisure.

Our Programmes

Based on our experience and research since 2013, we have developed many programmes at Rubaroo with the institutional partnerships that we have had. While the values of all programmes remain core to what we do, the methodology has been adapted to various classrooms, spaces, and communities. To nurture the ecosystem of young people, we have developed three categories of programmes—with youth, adolescents, and influencers of young people. The design of the programmes under each category is extremely unique from an experiential learning viewpoint. The involvement and co-creation of design along with multiple stakeholders involved distinguished it. Some of the themes around which we have developed programmes are:

Early and child marriage: Over the past three years, Rubaroo supported by American Jewish World Service (AJWS) and Pravah has worked with more than 300 adolescents from eight low-cost/under-resourced schools where the adolescents build their dreams and aspirations while also learning to negotiate with different stakeholders such as parents, teachers, and friends. The programme is an intensive leadership journey that addresses the issue of early and child marriage from a needs perspective of an individual.

Rural and sustainable development: Rubaroo every year takes students on an intensive 1-week orientation camp in rural Andhra Pradesh, preparing them for a month-long internship in different grassroots-level organisations to understand and contribute to developmental work. This exercise has contributed to mindset change, extensive understanding of developmental work in India, in-depth understanding of ground realities, and shift in utilisation of resources in the communities at large.

Empowering young global citizens (EYGC): EYGC was a leadership journey with high school students to analyse the role of media, understand their identity, and the influence of it in society and individual's lives. The participants questioned identity-based discrimination to create an interfaith world, where they also led social change projects within their institutions and communities. A curriculum was also developed on the issue of interfaith and working with adolescents through this programme.

A programme designed with the support of American consulate in Hyderabad to work with more than 100 students holding a dialogue on understanding perspectives of different faiths, engaging in a discussion with adolescents on practices and stereotypes.

Gender: In schools, Rubaroo conducts gender sensitisation sessions with adolescents addressing stereotypes. Rubaroo also works with adolescents, both boys and girls, on sexual and reproductive health rights.

Agaaz-e-Baatcheet: A call to 'initiate a conversation' on interfaith. Participants from diverse colleges across Hyderabad were part of a learning and leadership initiative to experience and understand multi-religious identities. They also lead Social Action Projects across diverse parts of the country. What has been the success? EYGC gave adolesc unique opportunity to have a dialogue around religion and handed-down identity. These workshops impact girls and boys differently; our success has been that both are able to voice their doubts and question a belief system handed down in the family from one generation to another. They need neutral spaces to do so and in fulfilling that need is Rubaroo's achievement. For example, we ran a project to showcase how media (WhatsApp, newspaper, and Facebook) share false news and how can we identify 'real news'. The social action project, which the students led, was comparing similar news coverage and their interpretations across different newspapers to analyse how each one had (mis)interpreted it differently. This gave adolescents a keen insight and a valuable lesson, which they spread across the board. In November 2017, another interfaith project was undertaken. Comprising 125 Youth Champions who reached out to 2,500 adolescents, through their Social Action Projects, were The Youth Champions—a group of extremely spirited young people who within a span of 2 months explored issues of identity-based discrimination. Supported by research, the Social Action Projects through diverse media—online and offline—spread communal harmony across Hyderabad. They held interviews, led peace walks, conversations, theatre, sessions, and workshops among many other activities to influence mindset change among adolescents and youth. Our partnerships have been forged towards long-term relationships because institutions have been able to see a shift and change within students that have participated in Rubaroo workshops. Parents and teachers have vouched for the way the participants saw conflicts in day-to-day life and negotiated different things in their own spaces. Multiple cases of child marriages and violence at home came out during the workshops, which were addressed with suitable interventions from schools, parents, and religious leaders. Rubaroo has been able to initiate dialogue between adolescents from diverse religious, faith, gender, socio-economic, and cultural backgrounds. Consequently, it has led to confidence building across diverse groups and in particular led to breaking barriers of mistrust due to identity conflict perpetuated due to sensationalism, social media, and television.

'Through this session I have interacted with a Muslim for the first time in my life.'

'I have understood that atheists aren't people that need to be despised.'

Peer Leaders

Every year, out of the 100 participants under our *My life – Mere faisle* (MLMF) programme, the programme facilitators choose 25 peer leaders from different school groups who have shown exceptional leadership skills by displaying ownership to the space, confidence, creating social bonds within the workshop space, and motivating peers by following and adhering to the values of the workshop. These leaders have negotiated within their spaces and have sought out to help their peers when in distress. From the peer leader group of 2016–17 batch, the young leaders underwent a theatre workshop for 3 days after which they came up with three plays, the stories penned, scripted, and enacted by them in public. Amongst the audience were principals, teachers, parents, and ordinary public who were visibly impressed by their highly endearing performances. These peer leaders are truly committed to the responsibility they carry and hold on to the values even after completion of the programme.

Overcoming our Challenges

Adolescent and youth work is person intensive. It essentially involves building relationships, empathy, and trust with participants to be able to influence positive mindset change. One of our initial struggles was working with the financials of the organisation because as much as there was a buy-in for the programmes that we were rolling out in Hyderabad, another challenge was also in these kinds of issues continued to prevail. As we aimed at challenging social norms, stereotypes, patriarchy, and existing societal patterns, it was difficult to work in communities where adolescents were challenging their influencers towards building their own aspirations and negotiating relationships with their stakeholders. The gender divide in classroom spaces were often not wanting to be challenged by institutions because of the deep-rooted fear of adolescents beginning to unleash 'change' that according to some was perceived as 'too much'. Slowly over time, as we began co-creating the designs and curriculums along with institutions, their buy-in would become stronger. Also, in due course of time, people began to understand where we were coming from and the kind of inclusion that we aimed to reach out for. Especially in under-resourced communities and schools, there often also would be many organisations who would want to create 'interventions' for adolescent groups. This became a challenge as the participant groups become audience to diverse range of programmes, each coming in from their understanding and perspective of change that they wanted to bring in. We began to also understand that we needed to work with them knowing the other programmes that the adolescents were a part of and ensuring that we integrated them together with the work that we were doing, such that they just did not become victims of everything that came their way but were able to take informed stances and decisions on things that mattered to them.

Learning from our Experiences

One of our learnings in our initial years was to understand the importance of working with influencers of adolescents and young people, instead of working with them in isolation. It became absolutely imperative to create an ecosystem for the adolescents and work with their stakeholders to see any sort of positive mindset change. As a consequence, it also then would become the responsibility of the ecosystem to work towards collective mindset change. In the ecosystem, more than anything, we realised the importance of working with women and mothers of adolescent groups because adolescents often tended to spend most time with them and are influenced by their values and choices through the behavioural patterns and values that they put in front of their children.

We also realised that short-term programmes only became a window for them to experience the possibilities of change, but for long-term learning and leadership, these programmes had to be an ongoing process to be sustainable and impactful. Any programme that we had to design also could not be run in isolation. The need was to be in sync with other programmes that the institutions catered to. It also was very important to pick up textbook curriculums and contextualise and juxtapose them to the social issues that we were addressing. The background, other programmes, and projects that may be a part of their schooling spaces was important in so much as they influenced their socio-economic well-being and were included in mentoring conversations. Adolescents also thrive in spaces of routine at home and institutions, and hence, planning their other schedules influence their being part of the programmes. Programmes should be negotiated for to be accommodated within their routine structures. While working with adolescents, the methodology that was needed was to connect outside classroom learning—exposures and visits within their institutional structures. It also needed to be fun, interactive, and something that they did not receive within their institutional spaces. Facilitators from outside their schooling spaces—a friend and mentor, without being just disciplinarians, with whom they could share without fear and with trust is important for adolescents. They also need everyday role models to look up to. Role models who not only inspire them to challenge themselves but enable each one to recognise their comfort zone and go beyond to do out-of-the-box thinking for maximum learning to happen. It is also very important for facilitators to sense their group's need of the moment, to modify the design to cater to the group's dynamics need in that particular moment. Workshop structures, as much as they may be pre-determined, should be receptive to participants' needs. Icebreakers often play a huge role in building rapport with participants.

Young people, hence, should be treated as adults and equals in decision-making while working with them, especially in our culture, which treats the young people as inexperienced and with scant respect. This becomes the foundation in building relationships with young people, and often the trust that they are given, that itself becomes an opportunity for them to shoulder responsibility and build better attitudes and values for them to understand their roles as active citizens across the world.

13

Agenda for Action

Conclusions and Recommendations

V.S. Vyas

Several pertinent issues raised in the papers in this volume deserve serious attention of all those concerned with the growth and development of adolescents, a key segment of our population. The issues are important not only because they are addressed to larger sections of the population but also because capabilities or lack of the present cohort of adolescents will define the character and strength of our country for years to come.

A number of case studies included in this volume have highlighted the issues arising from specific local contexts. They also present some meaningful and effective approaches used to face these issues. These should act as practical guidelines to cope with problems adolescents at large face and ways to nurture them into becoming responsible citizens.

These papers and studies were the basis of deliberations among the knowledgeable group of writers and some alert and articulate young boys and girls participating in the consultation on empowering adolescents. The attempt in this concluding summary is to present lessons drawn from these experiences and insights of the activists and scholars, as also suggestions on translating them into actions, both locally and nationally.

The lessons pertain to three critical dimensions, namely education, health, and citizenship.

Education

By all accounts, the present education system is the biggest obstacle to adolescent development. Some specific steps suggested to improve the situation include the following:

1. Adolescents should be classified into those who are part of the education system, those who have dropped out, and those who have not attended schools. Dropouts should be divided into two subgroups, those unable to compete with others and stay in the system and those who drop out for other socio-economic reasons. Distinct strategies for coping with educational issues of each group should be devised;
2. Programmes for dropouts discussed in this volume such as *Doosara Dasak* and that promoted by *Pratham* appear to be working. Their wider application, adapted to suit local conditions, should be considered;
3. Region-specific social mapping and micro-planning should be used to further education;
4. Community involvement in and ownership of education programmes should be strongly considered;
5. Local governments should be sensitised to concerns of adolescent development;
6. Ethical values as integral constituents of human nature should be taught, as *SIDH* does in its programme;
7. History, geography, and culture of the region should be important parts of education;
8. Alternative modes of education should be sympathetically examined as means to improve existing systems;
9. Family members should be continuously involved in adolescents' education;
10. The value of yoga, *pranayam*, meditation, music, and sports for wholesome development of adolescents should be

recognised, and they should become parts of the curriculum;

11. Computer and skill training should be introduced at appropriate stages;
12. Personality development, confidence building, and respect for physical labour should be parts of education;
13. Greater attention should be given to secondary education. Its extension and improvement of its quality should receive a high priority; and finally,
14. The main objective of education should be inculcating a spirit of enquiry in students.

Health

Ill health in its widest sense is the biggest impediment to adolescents' development. Some important measures for improving health are as follows:

1. The close relationship between education and health should be clearly recognised. Health awareness should be an important and essential part of education;
2. The integrated view on health should include reproductive, sexual, and nutritional aspects. Well-being and appropriate care should be parts of adolescents' health education;
3. The relatively high Indian maternal and child mortality rates suggest that *all* adolescents, and not just girls, need reproductive health education;
4. Adolescents should be facilitated to discuss their health-related issues with qualified counsellors;
5. The growing menace of substance abuse needs particular attention;
6. Civil society organisations and media need to be involved in health education, particularly in fighting evil social practices such as child marriage;
7. Adolescents should be made conscious that they are themselves responsible for their own health;

8. Parents need to be educated about health concerns of their children;
9. Health programmes should recognise diverse health needs of heterogeneous groups;
10. Various health-related programmes need to work synergistically, avoiding overlaps among them;
11. Attitudes of health care providers and programme executors are as important as their skills. Their training should emphasise the right attitudes;
12. Proper training and adequate resources should be provided to primary health workers engaged in adolescent health programmes; and
13. All school-going as well as non-school-going adolescents should be screened regularly for their health and counselled accordingly.

Citizenship

The ultimate objective of adolescent development is to nurture them into responsible citizens. Suggestions to achieve this include the following:

1. Adolescents should be exposed to values enshrined in the directive principles of the constitution at home (by parents) as well as in schools and other institutions;
2. They should also be taught to respect human rights and to protest against injustice and evil social practices;
3. They should be assigned roles in social movements;
4. Adolescents have the energy to bring about change and hence must be prepared for being change agents;
5. They should be taught to be responsible for their own well-being and good behaviour;
6. They should be familiarised with their immediate environment and become respectful of their culture and heritage;

7. They should be encouraged to engage in interfaith dialogues and appreciate diversity of our society;
8. They should be provided space for self-realisation as well as socialisation on their own terms, as advocated in the *Pravah* paper; and
9. Adolescents should not be treated merely as target groups for various schemes and programmes but more as active participants.

Implementation

These recommendations must not remain pious hopes. Papers presented at the consultation and their discussion led to concrete suggestions for implementation of these recommendations by two principal stakeholders, namely concerned governmental agencies and civil society institutions.

Government Agencies

1. A common definition of adolescents should be accepted by all different agencies;
2. Adolescent development goals may be dovetailed with the UN Sustainable Goals;
3. Policies and programmes affecting adolescents should recognise the changing features of modern youth as well as the environment impacting them;
4. They should be geared to specific goals and benchmarks, according to specific geographies and accompanied by timelines;
5. All programmes should provide greater attention to deprived sections and backward regions;
6. A model for participation of both government and civil society institutions working for the same purpose may be evolved;
7. An inter-agency group with a nodal department may be constituted in the government to look into issues affecting adolescents;

8. Efforts should be made to involve media for advocacy purposes;
9. Positive features of social media should be explored for empowering adolescents; and
10. These recommendations of the consultation on empowering adolescents in regard to education, health, and citizenship should form the core of state policy for adolescents.

Civil Society Institutions

1. A network of NGOs working with youth may be formed. It should attempt to build partnerships with government, media, academics, and subject matter specialists;
2. A continuing discussion of issues facing adolescents among all stakeholders is needed;
3. Strategies to scale up innovative NGO initiatives in education, health, and social issues should be developed;
4. NGOs should ensure transparent functioning and strict accountability to all stakeholders; and
5. Bigger NGOs should act as mentors to smaller institutions.

Index